D1309564

Garden Talk
Member Tips & Advice

NATIONAL HOME
GARDENING CLUB

Credits

Garden Talk — Member Tips & Advice

Tom Carpenter
Creative Director

Julie Cisler
Design and Production

Michele Stockham
Senior Book Development Coordinator

Justin Hancock
Editor

Gina Germ
Becky Fitch
Photo Editors

Photographers:
Michael Hendricks
Walt Chandoha
Chuck and Barbara Crandall
Jim Block
Derek Fell
Dave Brus/NHGC
Michael Landis/NHGC
Jeff Johnson/NHGC
Mowers Photography/NHGC

Illustrators:
Bill Reynolds
Bill Reynolds/K and K Studios
Nancy Wirsig McClure/Hand-to-Mouse Arts

A special thanks to all the members who also submitted photos and illustrations.

2 3 4 5 6 7 / 07 06 05 04 03
ISBN 1-58159-055-5

National Home Gardening Club
12301 Whitewater Drive
Minnetonka, MN 55343
www.gardeningclub.com

Contents

Welcome to *Garden Talk!* It's like a friendly visit over the back fence, filled with gardening *Tips & Advice.*

Across our great country, from coolest North to sultry South and from arid West to forested East, gardeners experience similar challenges and successes. These experiences run a range of emotions—anticipation for the first fruit or flower of the season, disappointment after a big wind knocks over a prized specimen, pride when your garden gets a compliment, and much more.

But no matter where you live, it seems there's always a need for solutions to problems, and ideas for making your garden even more beautiful and your work even easier. Your problem might be as little as a rabbit, as pesky as a deer, or as huge as a moose (believe it or not, they can be a garden pest!). Or perhaps it's an infestation of white flies, poor soil that needs amending, or a poorly-drained area that needs to dry out. On the other hand, you might just want ideas—how to keep weeds down, what to grow in that hot and sunny spot, the best flowers for attracting birds and butterflies.

NHGC members were kind enough to share their solutions and ideas in this book, *Garden Talk—Member Tips & Advice.* We call it *Garden Talk* because that's what it's like—a conversation over the back fence, a sharing of ideas and advice the likes of which you'll find nowhere else.

This book is packed with all sorts of homegrown wisdom. Though the ideas may not be "mainstream" or conform to traditional gardening practices, who cares! We have yet to see an Official Gardening Rule Book, and if an idea worked for somebody else it might work for you too! In fact, the hardest part about creating this book was paring down the number of tips and ideas we could include; NHGC members are that good and smart about gardening.

Remember—there are no guarantees in gardening. That's the challenge in the first place! So what worked for someone else, even your neighbor, may not work for you. But give these ideas a try— you're sure to find some of value. And that's as good advice as you get over the back fence in a talk about gardening with a neighbor or friend.

Good luck in all your gardening endeavors. May *Garden Talk* keep you trying new solutions and ideas, and expanding your gardening skills!

Justin Hancock

Justin Hancock loves horticulture and gardening more than anything else. As horticulture editor for *Gardening How-To* and other NHGC publications, he gets to share his passion with Club members like you.

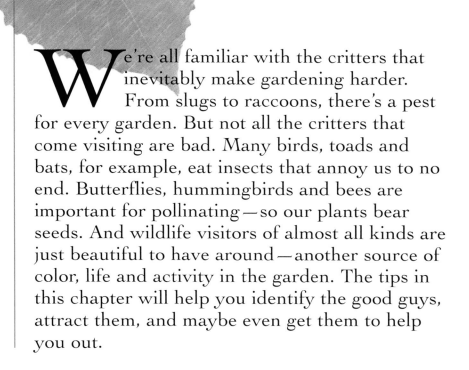

Chapter 1
Attracting Friendly Critters to the Garden

We're all familiar with the critters that inevitably make gardening harder. From slugs to raccoons, there's a pest for every garden. But not all the critters that come visiting are bad. Many birds, toads and bats, for example, eat insects that annoy us to no end. Butterflies, hummingbirds and bees are important for pollinating—so our plants bear seeds. And wildlife visitors of almost all kinds are just beautiful to have around—another source of color, life and activity in the garden. The tips in this chapter will help you identify the good guys, attract them, and maybe even get them to help you out.

Toads are big eaters of garden pests. They're even said to eat slugs. To attract these good guys, build a toad house.

How to Attract Insect-Eating Toads

To make a place for toads to come and live in your garden, dig a shallow hole, take the rocks out, mix some potting soil, take two rocks and put them on each side. Then put a flat piece of flagstone on top and a couple of clumps of sod behind the opening. Toads will come here and then they'll eat the bad bugs that cause all kinds of problems in your garden.

Ethel Singer
Sugar Run, Pennsylvania

Buy a Bat House!

Don't forget the benefit of bats. Bat houses help attract them—and bats eat lots and lots of bugs from the garden. Bats are especially good at eating mosquitoes.

Ann Bigger
Manton, Michigan

WILDLIFE

How an Old Pair of Boots Can Get Rid of Insects

To help attract wrens to my yard to eat insects, I hung some old work boots around my garden for them to nest in. The wrens really help keep the insects at bay (especially mosquitoes!) and have a lovely song.

Floyd Aleshire
Abbeville, Louisiana

Insect-eating birds work as natural pest control in your garden. They'll also entertain you with their antics and songs.

A Peanut Butter Bird Feeder

To make a fun bird feeder, take old 3-inch-wide hardwood branches that are about a foot long (I like to use maple, but you can use any kind you have). Drill 1-inch holes around the log in six to eight different spots. Fill these holes with some crunchy peanut butter (and mix in some birdseed, if you like). Drill a hole all the way through in the very top, thread a string, then hang the feeder from a tree branch.

Marcia Henderson
Independence, Iowa

An alternative to a cut Christmas tree: Use a potted tree and then plant it outside come spring. Look what it can grow into!

Oh, Christmas Tree

Do you hate the thought of throwing out your Christmas tree? Why not save it through the winter? If you leave it outside in your yard, it will provide shelter for the birds—they love flying in and out of it. Then in the summer when they have other shelter, you can chop it up and add it to your compost pile, where it will enrich your garden in years to come.

Diana Murrer
Rochester, New York

Make a Birdhouse

Empty orange juice containers make great birdhouses. If you take a quarter and trace a hole and cut into it near the bottom, you can make a great nesting spot for all kinds of different birds. (Be sure to make some small holes in the bottom for waste to run out of.) I found wrens in mine—and wrens love mosquitoes.

Ethel Singer
Sugar Run,
Pennsylvania

Friendly Finches

Want to attract finches to your garden? To make a thistle feeder for these birds, I take an old dish soap bottle and recycle it. Just wash it out well, dry it, then fill it with thistle seed. Put a small hole on each side near the bottom and insert a small dowel through the bottle below the holes; then hang it from the tree. The finches love it and so will your pocketbook.

Gordon
Weichers
Steamboat
Rock, Iowa

Thistle feeders will attract beautiful goldfinches.

GARDEN TALK

From the NHGC Staff...

Sensational Sunflowers

Expect to see plenty of bees on any sunflower during the first few days after the blossom opens. Three weeks later, as the seeds begin to ripen, finches and many other birds will promptly harvest them. Or you can cut the ripe old blossoms and save them for winter bird feeding. Sunflower seeds are ripe when the seeds fall out freely when you gently twist the dried flower. Also cut and save faded seed heads from the purple coneflowers you grow for butterflies. Birds love them!

Making Your Suction Cup Feeder Stick

If you use suction cups to hold things to your windows (such as bird feeders, thermometers, sun catchers, or that sort of thing), but have had a problem with the cups falling off your windows, just wash and dry the cups. Then rub them on your face and stick them on the window. (The facial oils help them stick better.) One thing to keep in mind is that suction cups do weather and wear out, so they need to be replaced eventually.

Marcia Henderson
Independence, Iowa

Homemade Birdbath Idea

Birdbaths can be very expensive, but I found a way to make them more cheaply. Just purchase several sizes of clay pots and stack them together with the top of the pot on the ground. Use some silicone to help them stick together and then use silicone to secure a large saucer on the top. The natural terra-cotta color looks natural in the garden, too.

Pat Stidham
Springboro, Ohio

Don't Get Stumped!

I lost a large blue spruce in my yard. Since it was so expensive to have the roots removed, I had it chopped down, but left a 12-foot stump. This became the focal point of my perennial border. Since I couldn't leave the giant stump, I had to come up with a way to decorate it. My solution was to put 10 birdhouses up on the stump. It's a great apartment building for birds!

Lynn Trump
Myerstown,
Pennsylvania

If you'd like a specific kind of bird to nest in your yard, do some research ahead of time. Different birds prefer different living conditions. The size of the entry hole makes a big difference. So does what—if anything—you put inside the nestbox. For instance, wrens like an empty box they can stuff full of twigs themselves; chickadees like some wood shavings inside from the start.

GARDEN TALK

Keep Your Window Box Going Through the Seasons

After cleaning out my window boxes for the year, I started to clean up my flower beds. I was on my way to the compost pile when I looked up at my now bare window boxes and suddenly decided to use all of the old seed heads from my flower beds to decorate them. Later, birds landed and ate all of the seeds I had used. A couple of seeds had fallen into the soil below and sprouted—so I even got more plants out of it!

Lora Rasor
Pleasant Hill, Ohio

For a More Natural Look

I use old woody vines to tie around the poles holding up my birdfeeders. These vines give the birds something to land on as they eat and help make the poles look more natural in my yard.

Lora Rasor
Pleasant Hill, Ohio

Food Court Is for the Birds

For all you avid bird watchers out there, here's a simple structure you can build to attract a host of bird species. My bird food court is composed of a simple wooden roof structure at a 45° pitch built from 2 x 4s and covered with exterior-grade plywood and shingles. The roof is supported by 4 x 4 pressure-treated posts, with a pipe running across the posts to hold up all of my bird feeders. The sheltered design keeps the birdseed dry.

I went to our nearest home improvement center and bought all of the necessary materials to build it. My husband, Bruce, built it according to what I had in mind for our backyard.

An added bonus of the project happens in late spring, when the area around the feeders becomes a whole circle of sunflowers that grow from fallen seed. It's beautiful. I love watching the flowers bloom in the backyard and the birds love it even more.

Rose and Bruce Harned
Southington, Ohio

From the NHGC Staff...

Bring on the Birds

Chickadees, bluebirds, warblers, some native sparrows and many other birds will actively patrol your garden for pests if you invite them in. Although these birds also eat seeds and fruits, in summer they especially crave extra protein to nourish growing nestlings; this protein is available from insects. To make birds feel welcome, place perches throughout your garden. These can be tomato cages or other wire structures that stand about 5 feet high—the perfect height for watchful birds in search of a creeping, crawling meal.

Use Native Plants

To help encourage wildlife to come to your yard, plant lots of native plants. The animals you want to attract should recognize these plants faster than others from far-away places. Various shrubs can help encourage birds by providing shelter. Fruiting shrubs are even better to help feed the flying critters. A birdbath also helps.

Maryjane Parry
Port Charlotte, Florida

Attract Bees to the Vegetable Garden

Plant flowers that bees love with your vegetables to encourage pollination. Cockscomb is a great choice here; bees love it. The seeds are very easy to start—just plant them in the soil and they'll grow.

Annie Wood
Roslyn, Pennsylvania

While ornamental flowers are most common for attracting bees and other pollinators, some vegetables, such as okra, do the job equally as well.

If sunflowers are too big for your garden, consider black-eyed Susans. Bees love the flowers and birds enjoy the seeds.

Add Some Color

Try planting early spring vegetables with sunflowers. By the time the sunflowers get big, the cool-season crops are done. Then in the summer, the sunflowers attract birds and bees to pollinate your vegetables. In the fall, you can harvest the seeds for yourself or save them to attract birds.

L. Decker
Clymer, Pennsylvania

Bird Feeder with a Five-Star Rating

I designed this bird feeder for my sister-in-law in Charleston, South Carolina. I added a unique endurance feature to help the feeder withstand the elements: I slipped carefully hand-fitted square rings of wood over the main torso of the feeder. It's mounted in the rock garden in the backyard.

Phil Duck
Columbia, South Carolina

Chapter 2
Vines and Trellises

No gardener should be without a vine. From the smallest balcony to a several acre garden, vines add special accents with their upright growth and variety of colors and textures. Some, such as scarlet runner beans, look ornamental and are edible at the same time. So go ahead. Try something new. Grow vines! Here's how.

GARDEN TALK

Use grapevines as supports for other plants. The look is great and natural, and the cost is right, too: free!

Support for Your Plants

I use wild grapevines as a support for my plants, instead of wire frames or strings. The grapevine looks a lot more natural and is much cheaper.

Liz McDonald
Fort Edward, New York

Start the Day Out Right

Train morning glories to climb up and around your favorite statue. It's a simple and fun way to make yourself smile when you look outside in the morning. If you have statues of people, it looks like they're peeking out from behind the plants at you.

Juliana Benoit
Easley, South Carolina

Try This for Your Beans

Does planting pole beans seem like a big chore? Here's an easy way. All you need to do to grow your pole beans without big poles is to plant a row of beans (or two rows a foot apart) and put up posts. Then stretch wire across the top of the posts. I use barley twine tied to the posts. Then string the twine from the wire on top to the string on bottom. The beans will climb up the strings. This makes it easy to harvest on both sides, and you can plant different bean varieties, too. When the beans are done, just take down the string and use that part of the garden for something else.

Larry Steele
Nallen, West Virginia

From the NHGC Staff...

Vines

Vines are often described as the "walls" of the garden, for they have the ability to decorate vertical surfaces on their climb up to the light. They soften and clothe walls, fences and the sides of buildings as they go. You can use vines to throw a green covering over an unsightly outbuilding, to beautify a neighbor's scratchy fence or add a veneer of civilization over a pile of rubble.

Vines can be either deciduous or evergreen. So if you wish to use a vine to create privacy, consider an evergreen type for year-round effect. There is good variety within the category of vines, with everything from dainty vines running up a string in a container, to spreading types that grow to 30 feet long, rambling over everything in their path. You can choose a vine that will be covered with fragrant blossoms, one with leaves that turn red and purple in the fall, even ones with berries for the birds.

You can use any number of supports to help grow climbing vegetables such as peas or beans.

GARDEN TALK

Color in Summer and Autumn

Do you have a small yard? If so, you don't have to count out vining crops like gourds or mini-pumpkins. You can plant these vegetables at the base of a strong trellis. If you guide the vines as they grow, you'll have a nice display, both from their beautiful flowers and from the colorful fruits they form.

Greg Wilke
Parkers Prairie, Minnesota

Here's a Way to Plant Beans

Here's how I grow green beans, even in a small spot. I just take a length of wire mesh fencing and secure it to a good, sturdy support that leans up at an angle. (In my case, I nailed mine to the eave of the house.) Plant your beans along the mesh fencing. It also makes them easy to pick because the heavy green beans will hang down through the fencing where you can see them.

Karen Carlton
Manhattan, Montana

You can grow ornamental vines the same way you would climbing vegetables if you'd like to dress up your vegetable garden.

Make Your Own Trellis

Trellises can be very expensive from the store, so I devised a way to make one inexpensively. I just drove galvanized nails and used nylon-braided string to make a trellis on the side of a building. You can tie the braided string in whatever designs you like for your climbing roses, morning glories, clematis or other vines to climb on.

Denise Williams
Central Square,
Florida

Roses look elegant no matter what they're growing on—from a fancy pergola to a simple trellis.

An Inexpensive Trellis Idea

I made a trellis for my black-eyed Susan vine by taking a large tomato cage and turning it upside down. I pulled the legs together and tied them with string. The vine climbed up the cage and soon covered it, making a beautiful display.

Gayle Stafford
Vardaman, Mississippi

GARDEN TALK

Add Color to Your Garden

To add a special touch to my garden, I wrapped white Christmas lights around my arched garden trellis. It looks so beautiful and our garden just glows at night with the soft lighting. It especially accentuates the pink jasmine on the trellis.

Tina
Via Internet

Make Your Trellis Last Longer

Here's how to help save your trellises from rotting off and getting ruined when you stick them in the ground. All you have to do is buy some conduit pipe. Then flatten one end of the pipe with a hammer. Once you have the end all sealed, insert the bottoms of your trellis in the open ends of the pipe, and stick it into the ground. The pipe protects your wood from rotting, and no one will even know it's there!

Judith Vancil
Westerville, Ohio

1 Take a metal conduit pipe and carefully close off the end with a hammer.

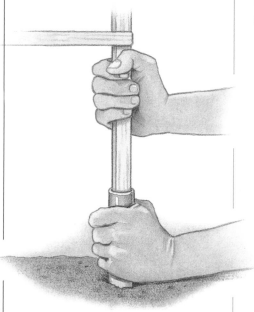

2 Then insert your trellis into the open end of the pipe.

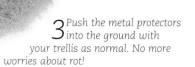

3 Push the metal protectors into the ground with your trellis as normal. No more worries about rot!

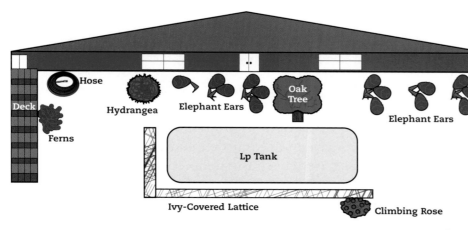

Hose
Deck
Ferns
Hydrangea
Elephant Ears
Oak Tree
Lp Tank
Elephant Ears
Ivy-Covered Lattice
Climbing Rose

Use plants to help cover potential eyesores in your yard. It's that simple! But you have to plan, and select a plant that will do the job.

Hiding a Propane Tank

I have a big propane tank in my yard. To cover it up, I placed a trellis partially around it and grew vines on the trellis. It has proven to be a very low-cost and low-maintenance solution. Plus, I got to plant more plants because of it, and add more color to my yard!

India Munden
Mobile, Alabama

Recycling to Make a Trellis

Want a cheap way to make a trellis? A friend and I built a combination trellis/blocking screen out of discarded wooden shutters from a salvage yard. We made a frame for it out of 2 x 4s and 4 x 4 posts, then nailed the shutters to the frame. You can grow plants on it or paint designs on the shutters to make them look even more ornamental.

Jerome Beder
Mukwonago, Wisconsin

Use Your Grapes

Everything in the garden has its use, even old woody grapevine trimmings. If you save them over the winter, you can make a tripod- or pyramid-shape out of old wooden broom handles, garden stakes, bamboo poles or sticks. Then just secure the poles together at the top, drive the bases into the ground, then wrap each pole with some grapevine. Vining plants will have lots of tendrils to climb up on.

Susan Carter
Richmond, Ohio

Cover that Chainlink Fence

I plant self-seeding vines (such as cherry tomatoes and malabar spinach) on my chainlink fence. It's very easy since I don't have to plant them every year and they help cover up the look of the chainlink. They give me more privacy, too, since my neighbors can't see through the vines.

Teri Caddle
Clayton, Illinois

Don't forget about climbing vegetables—they'll provide joy to your taste buds and your eyes.

Trellis Breathing Room

Putting up a new trellis? If you put it up against a building, be sure to leave room between your trellis and the wall. This will help your plants grow up around the trellis more easily and help preserve the surface of the wall. (If there's not enough air flow between the trellis and the wall, you might have problems with wood rotting.) What I do to keep a good distance is nail old thread spools to the side of the wall. Then I nail my trellis onto the spools. No one knows the spools are even there.

Dorothy Hancock Detroit Lakes, Minnesota

Trellises can be freestanding or supported by a wall, building or other structure.

Climb the Ladder

I have a small backyard and not enough room for the garden I want. I really wanted to grow gourds for birdhouses, though, so I figured out a way. Here's how. I used an old wooden stepladder, dug it in the ground a few inches so it would be sturdy and planted the seeds of my gourds underneath. The vines climbed right up to the top and covered the ladder!

Vicky Forster
Lidgerwood, North Dakota

Vines, Vines, and More Vines

For an interesting change try several different vining plants together on a single trellis or fence. It really helps to choose vines with complimentary colors and different leaf shapes. One example that I like is cardinal climber (*Ipomoea* x *multifida* 'Cardinalis'), Cypress vine (*Ipomoea quamoclit*) and morning glory 'Star of Yelta'.

Amy Neigebauer
Owatonna, Minnesota

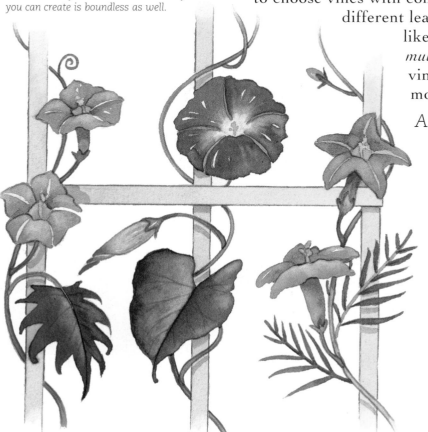

Use a variety of vines in your garden. The choice is nearly endless! And the beauty you can create is boundless as well.

Arbor Goes Up Better with Teamwork

This arbor makes an attractive entrance to our rear deck. My husband and I saw a smaller version of the arbor while we were on a walk one day, and we thought it would make a good trellis for our fast-growing trumpet vine.

We used 4 x 4 posts and two 1 x 8s with half moons cut from their centers to make the archway. I enjoy the oriental appearance of this feature. We decided to use vinyl lattice since our cold, wet winters, along with the ground heaving up, can be terribly hard on wood lattice. The color we chose for the lattice contrasts nicely to the cherry stain we used on the pine wood. The 4 x 4s are lag-bolted to the deck rails for extra support.

This arbor makes an inviting entrance to the deck.

My husband and I completed the entire arbor in a weekend for under $100. I've always enjoyed working on outdoor projects, and it seems that the more I do, the more my husband, Ken, enjoys teaming up on our ideas.

Joy and Ken Mott
Sandpoint, Idaho

Chapter 3
Keeping Critters Out of the Garden

Just about every gardener has had to deal with a "bad" critter of some sort. From moles and gophers to squirrels, raccoons and deer, there are creatures we just don't want to share our plants with. Deterring the pests usually isn't easy; it seems like our animal friends are often as smart—or smarter—than we are! So this section is full of ideas on how to keep them out. Remember: what works for one gardener might not work for another. Take these tips on a trial-and-error basis, but by all means give them a try!

From the NHGC Staff...

Good Critters

Here is a partial list of creatures that gobble up bugs harmful to your plants, or pollinate plants ... "good critters" you'll welcome into your garden.

Lady Bug Beetles: Eat mealybugs, scale, whiteflies and mites.

Lacewings: Eat aphids, mealybugs, scale, whiteflies and mites.

Syrphid Flies: Eat aphids, mealybugs, scale and whiteflies.

Soldier Beetles: Eat cutworms, gypsy moth larvae, cankerworms, snails and slugs.

Praying Mantis (can be purchased): Eats anything it can catch.

Wasps and Yellow Jackets: Eat small caterpillars.

Bees and Bumble Bees: Pollinate trees and plants.

Spiders: Eat anything that lands in their web.

Birds: Many nesting birds eat huge amounts of insects and caterpillars.

Keep Birds from Your Strawberries

I find small rocks about the size of strawberries and paint them red. I put these in my strawberry patch to attract the birds to keep the birds from eating my strawberries. I also take tape from an old VCR or cassette tape and crisscross it from stakes in the patch. The tape's fluttering, moving and flashing activity scares the birds and keeps them away.

David Hutchison
Monticello, Kentucky

Protect Young Plants

I stick $1^{1}/_{2}$- to 2-inch PVC pipe into the ground on each side of a plant when I plant it. Then I make a circle out of wire around the two pieces of pipe to help protect my tender young plants from animals. When the plants are tougher, just pull the PVC up over the plant.

Roland Anderson
Loughman, Florida

Don't Let Critters Make Lunch Out of Your Bulbs

Squirrels and other critters love to wreak havoc with my bulbs. Then I found out how to stop them. To protect bulbs when you plant them, lay some chicken wire around the sides of the bulbs. This will help protect them since the animals can't dig through the wire, but the plants can still grow through it.

Marcella Hazelrigg
Chesterfield,
South Carolina

"Plant" Pepper with Your Bulbs

Have problems with squirrels and other critters attacking your bulbs? If so, try "planting" some cayenne pepper powder in the soil with your bulb. One taste and the critters will run away every time, leaving your bulbs alone.

Jeanette Reinhardt
Little Falls, New York

Hot pepper has many uses for deterring garden pests.

Stopping Rabbits

Do you have a problem with rabbits? I used to. If you put rabbit feeders in your yard away from your gardens, they'll eat the feed that you put out for them and leave your flowers alone.

Ethel Singer
Sugar Run, Pennsylvania

How to Outsmart Cabbage Moths

Do you have problems with cabbage moths eating your broccoli and other crops? If so, just plant them in the fall—the moths are all gone by the end of the season. And you'll have a second crop of wonderful, fresh produce when usually there is none coming from your garden!

William Judkins
Greenwood, Indiana

Plant some cool-season vegetables in late summer or early autumn for a delicious second harvest ... and to better avoid cabbage moths.

Protect Your Trees

I've had a problem with rabbits eating the bark off of my fruit trees during the winter. I stopped them by buying some PVC pipe and cutting it lengthwise down the center. I can pull it open and wrap it around my trees. Then in spring I can open it back up and take it off. The pipe comes in a variety of sizes, for different-sized trees.

Richard Sowers
East Bertin, Pennsylvania

Stop Cutworms, Slugs and Others

Do your plants need protection from insect pests that live on the ground? I use cardboard tubes from paper towels or bathroom tissue to stop cutworms and slugs from attacking plants. All I do is cut the tubes into 2- or 3-inch lengths. I slip the tube over the plant and partially into the ground, creating a barrier. In the fall, you can just dig the tubes into the ground where they'll biodegrade.

James Dolweck
Greensboro, North Carolina

Advice *from the* Editor

Keep Cats Out

If you have problems with cats in your garden, lay some chicken wire on the soil surface and lightly cover it with mulch. Since the cats won't be able to "scratch" the soil, they should go someplace else.

There are many homegrown strategies for keeping slugs at bay. You might need to try several—or combinations of more than one—before you find one that works for you.

Soap-and-pepper sprays control aphids, and many other soft-bodied insects as well.

A Homemade Spray

I use a combination of one clove garlic, a small onion, a teaspoon of cayenne pepper and a tablespoon of liquid dish soap in a quart of water to control aphids in my garden. Put the ingredients in a blender and then boil them on the stove. Strain out the solids after the mix is cool, and pour it into a plastic spray bottle. All the ingredients are safe, so I don't have to worry about them.

Amy Lindsay
McMinnville, Oregon

A Green, Growing Fence

Do you have a problem with neighbor children or animals crossing your yard? I did until I put in a row of black raspberries. The thorny plants kept children and animals from the yard and gave us fruit that we love. It's so great to harvest fresh black raspberries!

Carol Lee Bohannan
Topeka, Kansas

"Pepper" Corn

Put cayenne pepper on the silks of your sweet corn, when the silks first appear. Repeat it after each rain. It's a very effective way to protect your corn from marauding raccoons. My neighbors lost their whole crop—I only lost two ears. The pepper is as hot to the raccoons as it is to people, so they stay away from it.

Joleta Deininger
Centerville, Iowa

Slug-Stopping

To deal with slugs, place a shallow pan of beer in your garden where slugs live. (I've found a pie plate works well.) Dig it in so it's even with the soil line. The slugs are attracted to the beer and climb in the dish. They will drown by morning. Then just throw out the beer and dead slugs and fill the dish back up.

Shari Hathaway
Brooklyn Park, Minnesota

Insects don't stop at munching in the garden—sometimes they'll munch on you, too. Mary Layton's lace clothes keep them at bay!

Mosquito Clothes

If you have a problem with mosquitoes in your garden, make lace clothes to wear when you're in the yard. I made lace pants from lace yard goods. They help you stay cool, too, because air can flow around your body better than if you wear long pants.

Mary Layton
King, North Carolina

Save Your Corn

Birds love to get at your sweet corn. If you don't stop them in time, they can take your whole crop—leaving you with nothing to show for all of your hard work through the season. To keep my corn safe, I take $1^{1}/_{2}$-inch strips of masking tape and wrap the end of each ear. Not only do the birds leave it alone (they can't peel the husks off), but you keep out bugs and worms, too.

David Hutchison
Monticello, Kentucky

Many garden critters like fresh sweet corn as much as you do.

Keep Birds Out of the Garden

You can recycle the old aluminum pie tins from the grocery store. Just punch a small hole in the bottom of them and string them to a pole or post. They'll blow around in the breeze, flapping and flashing. Birds don't like it, and will leave your garden alone.

Donna Lewis
Antwerp, New York

Whether it's the sound or flashing light, metal pie tins help deter birds.

An Ounce of Prevention...

Roses seem to need special attention—and they'll do best if you give it to them. I look over my roses every morning. If I detect a leaf with blackspot or another kind of problem, I simply remove it and destroy it. This helps stop the disease from spreading to the other leaves and petals. That, along with mulching well and only watering in the morning, is the best protection I know of to keep your roses healthy and disease free. It also helps with your other plants.

Sandra Arnett
Robertsdale, Alabama

They say an ounce of prevention is worth a pound of cure, and that's certainly true in the rose garden.

Besides human clothes, you might try using pet bedding that has a dog smell, to repel raccoons. These tricks can scare off deer, too.

Raccoon-Proofing Your Sweet Corn

Raccoons can demolish your sweet corn crop overnight. To stop them, I place small articles of dirty laundry, such as socks, on the stalks a night or two before the ears are ready to pick. The human scent keeps the critters away because they think you're in the garden guarding your corn.

Norma Musser
Womelsdorf, Pennsylvania

Recycling to Stop Cabbageworms

I used to have a problem with cabbageworms on my broccoli, cabbage and cauliflower. My solution is to use old pantyhose to cover the plant, then use a rubberband to hold the hose on the stem. That will allow the plant to grow because the nylon stretches as your plant grows, but butterflies can't lay their eggs on the plants.

Rod Piepho
Eagle Bend, Minnesota

Pantyhose—stretched over your broccoli, cabbage and cauliflower—will prevent butterflies from laying eggs there. This, in turn, will control cabbageworms.

CRITTERS

CRITTERS

Strong-smelling herbs and spices are said to repel insects. If cinnamon doesn't repel ants, try mint.

No Ants Allowed!

If you have a problem with ants getting in your house, take a bit of ground cinnamon and put it where the ants are coming in. For some reason, the cinnamon repels them. Try it, it works!

Barbara Workman
Auburn, Washington

What to Do About Ants

Have an ant problem? If so, make a mix of one package dry yeast, a quarter of a cup of honey, and enough water to make a paste. Spread this paste on 2-inch squares of cardboard and place where you suspect ants. It's safe, too, for children or pets.

Barbara Workman
Auburn, Washington

Advice *from the* Editor

Keep Insects Away

Don't wear the colors blue or yellow in the garden—insects are, in general, attracted to these two colors. Also, avoid wearing perfumes or colognes to attract fewer insects.

Woodpeckers are usually welcome in the garden, because they eat many pests. However, there are ways to keep woodpeckers away if you feel your beautiful trees—such as this maple— are threatened.

Stop Those Woodpeckers

I used to have a problem with woodpeckers knocking holes into two beautiful maple trees in my yard. I finally found a solution that worked. I just went to my sewing room and cut strips of cloth big enough to tie around the trees. I tied strips of cloth vertically between the two strips, leaving enough slack so that they'd move in the breeze. We never had another woodpecker on our maples. I think the woodpeckers thought they were giant snakes.

Sara Harrison
Easley, South Carolina

Cucumber Beetles

Do you have a problem with cucumber beetles attacking your plants? I used to, but then I found a solution. Take the aluminum pie tins you get from the bakery or grocery store and paint them the color of your cucumber blossoms. (It has to be as close to the same color yellow as you can get.) As soon as your cucumber plants sprout, set these on the ground. Fill the tins with water and a drop of dish soap. If you have the right shade of yellow, you'll catch cucumber beetles in droves.

Anita King
Greenwich, New York

Hate Raccoons?

Do raccoons love your sweet corn? Here's a surefire way to keep them out of your patch so you can enjoy your harvests. All you need to do is put a short electric wire close to the ground. There are some kits that even use solar power, so you don't have to use electricity!

Amber Morrow
Maplewood, Minnesota

Got Moles?

Moles can be a huge challenge to any gardener. Here's a way I've discovered to keep them at bay. All you have to do is place some human hair or pet hair in a mole hole. The scent deters all of those pesky moles from the garden or lawn.

Amber Morrow
Maplewood, Minnesota

Keep your sweet corn and other vegetables safe from raccoons by using electric fencing. If this doesn't work, try using fencing with some of the other tips suggested in this book.

Chapter 4

For the Vegetable Garden

Vegetable gardening is special—it's definitely got its own style. With no other kind of gardening are the results quite so tangible—especially in the depths of winter when you feast on homegrown veggies you canned earlier that autumn. But while vegetable gardening is fun and rewarding, it does have its share of challenges. That's what this section will help you overcome. These tips should help you get your best harvest ever!

Squash and pumpkins are related. Try using them in similar ways!

Too Much Squash?

Do you sometimes find that your vegetable plants produce too much? Mine have. I discovered that if you have extra butternut squash at the end of the season, you can use them in your pumpkin pie recipes, just substituting the squash for the pumpkins. No one will know the difference, the taste is outstanding, and you can freeze the pies to use through the year.

Mary Melcer
Bremond, Texas

Baskets of Cukes

Need to save space in your garden? Try planting your cucumbers in hanging baskets. They grow well there with proper care, and you can grow other vegetables in their place on the ground.

Julie Summers
Grayland, Washington

Use Your Milk Jugs

I have a tip on how to get a head start on the growing season while recycling a product I use. I recycle my milk jugs: Just cut off the tops, turn them upside down and use the "hot caps" to cover delicate plants (such as tomatoes) from freezing early in the spring. They let light in, but help keep the warmth of the sun in during the cooler nights.

Kathryn Miller
Ballantine, Michigan

For Your Herb Bed

I like to plant all my herbs together, but most need more water than my dill. I couldn't figure out what to do. Then I came up with a plan. Now I plant my dill plants on small hills in the center of my bed. Because the dill is higher up than the other plants, the roots stay drier like they need to, and at the same time, the other herbs get as much moisture as they need.

Heather Jackson
Taylorville, Illinois

Besides being useful in cooking, dill can do a good job attracting butterflies.

GARDEN TALK

Keep Your Lettuce Going

Here's a tip to get more bang for your buck from your lettuce patch. Try mixing together all your favorite types of lettuce. Then plant the seed mix so that your favorite varieties are all together in a spot. When you plant, only plant enough for a week's supply. Then a week later, plant another week's supply. Staggering your planting ensures you have lettuce for a longer time in the season and that there will be several varieties—all of which you like! You can do this in both spring and fall in most areas because lettuce likes cool weather. A fall planting will give you more fresh lettuce.

Rhonda Miller
Scottsburg, Indiana

What to Do with the Extras?

If you have lots of extra vegetables at the end of the season, consider donating some to a local food bank, homeless shelter or other charity. You can also sell the extras and donate the money to a charity. One great program is called Plant A Row for the Hungry.

Shari Hathaway
Brooklyn Park, Minnesota

Make Your Vegetable Garden Look as Good as Your Flower Beds

Gardening should be fun—adjust some of the "rules" to suit your specific tastes!

I've always admired formal knot gardens, but didn't have the space. I then figured out a way and incorporated the idea into my vegetable garden. Instead of boxwood, I planted carrots. You can substitute other vegetables for the other plants. It helps make your vegetable garden look much more ornamental, and even more fun to grow. Each season you can grow a different knot!

Barbara Morse
Greene, New York

Give to the Hungry

Try planting an extra row of vegetables in your garden if you have the space. In the fall, you can donate the fresh vegetables from the extra row to a food shelf. The food shelves really appreciate it—fresh vegetables!—and you can feel good about having helped others in need.

Edward Plihall
Hilliard, Ohio

What do you do with too many vegetables? Try donating them to others who don't have fresh vegetables.

GARDEN TALK

The gorgeous red roots aren't the only edible parts of a radish. Use the washed leaves to add pizzazz to salads, stir-fries and other dishes.

More than Just the Root

Save all your radish leaves to add some extra zing to your cooking. Just clean and chop the leaves, then throw them in with your other stir-fried vegetables. Radish leaves are not nearly as hot as the roots, and have a great flavor.

Jean Fields
Apple Valley, California

Planting Carrot Seed

When you plant your carrot seeds, mix them with sand. It helps thin the seeds out so you don't have to do it later on in the season.

Merill Monical
Hammond, Wisconsin

Use Old Shoelaces

When you have to throw away old shoes, save the laces. You can use them as plant ties for tomatoes, beans and other plants.

Marie Gussler
Lithopolis, Ohio

Raised Beds for Potatoes

I plant my potatoes in special containers made from old car or tractor tires. Take a tire and fill it with potting soil. You can stack more tires up as your plants get bigger. Then when it comes time to harvest, you can just remove all of the old tires. You don't have to dig any more!

Phoebe Meridith
Stilwell, Oklahoma

Plant potatoes in tires to save work! Another benefit: You can move the tires from place to place each year. This helps prevent diseases.

Potato Planting

Here's a tip to make planting potatoes a lot easier. Prepare your bed like normal, then put your potatoes about an inch or two in the ground. Instead of covering the potato piece, leave it exposed. Then cover the bed with 8 inches of weed-free hay. When it's harvest time, all you have to do is clear away the hay—no more digging. It's so much faster and easier! After you harvest, just dig the hay into the ground and let it decompose!

Bernadette Olfando
Whitetop, Virginia

Store Your Cucumbers Longer

Cucumbers are great, but after they're picked, they get soft really fast. I found a way to keep them crisp for much longer. Just wash them well and put them in a plastic grocery bag and put them in the refrigerator. They last for weeks.

Jean Oblinsky
Clymer, Pennsylvania

Be sure to clean vegetables thoroughly to help them last longer.

Homemade Greenhouses

Want to get a head start on the growing season? I found a quick and cheap way to make mini-greenhouses for my tender plants. All you have to do is take a plastic grocery bag and cut a 1-inch hole in the bottom. Lay this in your garden and plant your tomato plant in the hole. Then set plastic containers filled with water side by side, so your tomato sits between them. Just tie the handles of the bag loosely together and you have a mini-greenhouse. The sun will warm the water and then keep your plants warmer at night. Once the temperatures get warmer, just cut the plastic bag off and watch your plants grow!

Sophia Cameron
Hartly, Delaware

A plastic bag helps keep heat in when it's cool, but be sure to open it as the day warms up so your "greenhouse" doesn't trap too much heat.

Peppers or Tomatoes

I plant my tomatoes and peppers in concrete blocks. Just fill the two large holes in the blocks up with soil and plant away. In the fall, just pull your plants, soil and all, out of the holes. In spring, you can fill them back up and plant again.

Steven Wrotman
Rhinelander,
Wisconsin

Planting tomatoes "up" will also help prevent disease problems.

Peppers provide wonderful fruits, but they can be ornamental as well.

Save Your Peppers

If your pepper plants didn't produce well over the year, I have a method to give them another chance. In the fall, before frost, dig the plants up and put them in containers. Leave these containers in the cellar or some other place that it doesn't freeze. Plant your peppers next spring. They'll give you the biggest peppers you have ever grown. This has worked for me for many years.

Ed Lehsten
Buffalo, New York

Pollinating Tips

I pollinate my pumpkins, squashes and other plants. Just take a Q-tip and dust some yellow, powdery pollen from one flower onto the sticky part of another. Be sure to use a different Q-tip for each kind of plant. It's kind of fun and gives you a better harvest from your plants.

Sheri Nikolaus
Eureka, Montana

If you don't have bees or other pollinators to help, you might have to do the job yourself.

From the NHGC Staff...

Yields of Fruits and Vegetables (25-ft. rows)

Crop	Yield	Notes
Asparagus	8–10 lbs.	Over six-week harvest
Beans, Dry	25 lbs.	
Beans, Green	25 lbs.	For freezing and canning
Beans, Green	10 lbs.	Baby "filet" beans
Beets	25–35 lbs.	
Broccoli	25 lbs.	
Brussels Sprouts	5 lbs.	
Cabbage	40–50 lbs.	
Carrots	25 lbs.	For mature harvest
Carrots	15–20 lbs.	Baby carrots
Cauliflower	20–25 lbs.	
Celeriac	10–15 lbs.	
Celery	20–25 bchs.	
Cress	3–5 lbs.	
Cucumbers	25–35 lbs.	
Dandelion	3–5 lbs.	
Eggplant	20–25 lbs.	Less in cool climates
Endive	20–25 lbs.	
Garlic	40–50 bulbs	
Kale	25–40 lbs.	Multiple harvests
Kohlrabi	15–20 lbs.	
Leeks	20–25 lbs.	
Lettuce	15–20 lbs.	Left to mature
Lettuce	3–5 lbs.	Cut for mesclun
Mâche	3–5 lbs.	
Mustard	25–40 lbs.	Left to mature
Mustard	3–5 lbs.	Cut for mesclun
Onions	25–40 lbs.	
Parsnips	25–30 lbs.	
Peas	8–10 lbs.	
Peppers	10–20 lbs.	Less in cool climates
Potatoes	25 lbs.	
Pumpkins	50–75 lbs.	Depending on type
Radishes	8–10 lbs.	
Shallots	15–20 lbs.	
Spinach	10–20 lbs.	Depending on size at harvest
Squash, summer	5–25 lbs.	Depending on size at harvest
Squash, winter	35–40 lbs.	
Sweet Corn	25–30 ears	Plant at least four rows
Tomatoes	25–30 lbs.	
Turnips	15–25 lbs.	Depending on type

How many vegetables are too many for you? That's for you to decide, but this chart will help you know about how much you'll want to plant.

These yields assume high fertility and plant density.

Chapter 5
Seed-Starting Strategy

S tarting your plants from seed is like watching magic. In only a few months, a tiny speck of a seed can turn into a whole plant, complete with blooms and the start of another crop of seeds. But as wonderful as the activity is, there are plenty of pitfalls that stand between you and success. This chapter is filled with seed-starting advice handed down from experienced gardeners; the ideas here will help make your next seed-starting venture your best yet.

Here, an old pop bottle becomes a brand-new, miniature greenhouse!

Recycle Bottles

I recycle my plastic 1-liter bottles. Just cut the middle from the bottle and punch a few drainage holes in the bottom. Then use the top portion as the cover. They make great miniature greenhouses for your seedlings or small houseplants.

Rachael Owlett
Falls Chuch, Virginia

Save Your Back While Planting Seeds

Bending over repeatedly can be hard on your back at any age. I found that if I use a 4-foot-long piece of PVC pipe to help me plant my seeds, I can ease a lot of the strain. I just dig a furrow and place the pipe over the spot where I want my seeds. Then I all I have to do is drop each seed down the pipe. I like it best for bigger seeds like cucumbers and beans, but it works for all but the smallest kinds of seeds.

Diane Graves
Lisbon, New York

From the NHGC Staff...

Easy Plants for Saving Seeds

Flowers		Vegetables
Bachelor's button	Poppy	Arugula
Black-eyed Susan	Sunflower	Beans
Cleome	Sweet pea	Kale
Cosmos	Sweet William	Lettuce
Daisies	Zinnia	Okra
Hollyhock		Peas
Marigold		Pepper
Morning glory		Tomato

GROWING

Another Seed-Starting Plan

I save all my old plastic boxes from cakes and cookies that I get from the bakery, and use them for starting seeds. The clear plastic boxes have hinged lids that help conserve moisture and humidity when your seeds are sprouting. After the seedlings grow, you can take the lid off so they don't get fungal diseases from too much humidity and moisture.

Theresa Hassoch
Haskell, New Jersey

Try Your Seeds in Cups

I grow my seeds by planting them in little dixie cups. I poke holes in the bottom of the cups for the excess water to escape, then plant my seeds. I cover them by shaking a small amount of potting soil on them with a spoon. Keep the soil moist and before long you should see sprouts. While the seedlings are developing, you can leave them on a tray so it's easy to harden them off. (To do this, leave them outside for a while each day, so that they spend a bit more time outside each week.) Then when they're ready, just tear or cut off the cup and plant the seedling in your garden.

Kimberly Heibel
Leslie, Michigan

Advice *from the* Editor

For Better Luck With Cuttings

If you take stem cuttings from your plants, it's helpful to remove about a fourth of each leaf. This will help prevent the cutting from losing too much moisture through the leaves while it's trying to root.

You can start seeds in nearly any container—be creative! The seeds aren't fussy; you needn't be either.

Seeds form at the base of the flower. Wait to harvest them until after the flower has faded completely and the capsule becomes dry.

Seed Saving Success

You can collect the seeds from your annuals to plant next year. The seeds form in pods where the flowers used to be, before they faded. The seeds should be ready at the end of the season. You can save a lot of money if you don't have to buy new plants each year. (But remember. If you buy hybrid plants, the seeds probably won't grow into plants that look just like their parents.)

Marcella Hazelrigg
Chesterfield, South Carolina

Perennial Plan

When I plant my perennial seeds, I buy a mature plant to grow right next to them. You get to see the grown plant so it's easier to determine which are seedlings and which are weeds. It also gives you some full-grown color while your baby seedlings are developing.

Darlene Weiland
Mound, Minnesota

Planting perennial seedlings with mature plants can help give you color now and for years to come.

Use Old Chopsticks

Have you wondered what to do with old chopsticks, but couldn't find a use for them so you ended up throwing them away? Well you don't have to anymore. Save wooden chopsticks and use them as markers in your rows when you plant your seeds. The chopsticks' flat sides make it easy to write on them, too, if you want to!

June Garcia
Honokaa, Hawaii

Use chopsticks to mark where you planted bulbs.

What to Do with Old Windows

If you see old windows, be sure to recycle them. They make wonderful coldframes. Just lean them together in an "A" shape and brace the bottoms with bricks. They're portable, too. (Be very careful when you work with them, though, because older glass can often be extra fragile, and easily broken.)

Annie Wood
Roslyn, Pennsylvania

Advice *from the* Editor

Research is Good

Always know the requirements of a plant before you decide to plant it. If it won't grow well in your area, you should look for other plants that will. It hardly ever works to try to match the site to a plant. For instance, rhododendrons need acidic soil; if yours is alkaline, they won't grow.

Many plants have specific growing requirements. Be sure you know what they are before you plant.

GARDEN TALK

If you keep the seed packets you buy, you can store the tea bags inside them for easier seed identification.

Tea Bags

I use the outside covers of tea bags when I find seed to collect. These little bags make great temporary seed packets. I keep some with me all the time since I never know when I'll have the opportunity to collect some seeds!

Kurken Kirk
Kingston, New York

Seedling Markers

I use old popsicle sticks to mark what seeds or plants I've planted. Just write the name of the flower on the stick, then plant the stick at the edge of the hole. This helps me recognize new plants, as well as weeds.

Sharon Johnson
Pear River, Louisiana

Advice *from the* Editor

Transplanting Tip

Whenever you transplant a plant, it's very helpful to cut it back. This will help compensate for the damage that the root system endures while being moved.

Gardening Fans

Before we harden off our seedlings that we start outside, we place them in front of an oscillating fan for two hours in the morning and two hours in the evening. This helps strengthen them so they don't get damaged by the wind when we finally put them outside for good.

L. Decker
Clymer, Pennsylvania

Another Chopstick Lover

I like to use wooden chopsticks from restaurants for plant stakes. The chopsticks are free and work just as well as any kind of stake you purchase from the store. Plus, they're a neutral color, so they blend into your garden better than many other kinds of stakes.

Amy Peterson
Minneapolis, Minnesota

You need to give seedlings inside a chance to adjust to outside conditions before you plant them out. This process is called hardening off.

From the NHGC Staff...

Germination and Growing Temperature for Various Vegetable and Herb Transplants

Crop	Germ. Temp.* (F)	Days to Germ.	Growing Temp. (F)	Weeks to Transplant
Tomatoes	60–85	7–14	55–85	6–8
Eggplants	75–90	7–14	65–85	8–10
Peppers	65–95	7–14	65–85	8–10
Cabbage	45–95	4–12	55–75	4–6
Broccoli	45–85	4–12	55–75	4–6
Cauliflower	45–85	4–12	55–75	4–6
Brussels sprouts	45–85	4–12	55–75	4–6
Lettuce	40–80	2–14	55–75	2–4
Basil	65–85	7–14	65–85	8–10
Parsley	50–85	14–28	55–75	10–12
Onions	50–95	7–14	55–75	6–8
Leeks	50–95	7–14	55–75	6–8
Celeriac	60–70	7–14	55–75	10–12

*This chart lists the best temperature to start your seeds at, how long it takes for seeds to sprout when at these temperatures, and what temperatures are best to grow the plants at. It's usually best to have warmer daytime temperatures than nighttime ones.

GARDEN TALK

From the NHGC Staff...

Add Some Light

If your young plants lean toward their light source and look spindly and weak, they are not getting enough light. Hang grow lights or full-spectrum lights 4 to 6 inches above the containers for compact growth.

Make simple grow lights from fluorescent fixtures. Use full-spectrum lights, and raise them with ceiling hooks and chains as your plants grow.

Passive Heating

To help heat your coldframe when it's cold in the spring, take some old red bricks and leave them out in the sun all day long. During the day, the bricks absorb heat. In the evening when the temperatures start to cool, take your warm bricks and put them in your coldframe. They'll slowly release their heat and keep your plants warmer throughout the cool nights.

Rhonda Miller
Scottsburg, Indiana

Recycling to Start Seeds

You can use egg cartons to start seeds. Keep the seeds there until they grow large enough that you have to move them. You can use the Styrofoam kind of egg carton again and again, or use the paper kind once. The paper kind will eventually break down if you dig them into your soil.

Mary Miller
Hardin, Montana

Egg cartons are great for starting seeds, but you can also use the cardboard boxes you buy fruit in.

GROWING

Greenhouse on Wheels

I recently built a portable greenhouse. It has three shelves measuring 3 x 4 feet for a total of 36 square feet of space for nursery plants.

The unit is mounted on two fixed and two swivel caster wheels, so it can be easily moved into a garage or another enclosure when the temperature is low enough to endanger plants. I also included a small, portable ceramic heater.

The framework consists of 2 x 4s with 2 x 2s on the doors in the front, back and top. The shelves are ½-inch-diameter electrical thin-wall conduit, which provides good cross-ventilation. The screen-door hooks on the doors allow the doors to be closed or opened at various levels for ventilation. The whole unit is covered with reinforced greenhouse fabric, permitting good light penetration.

This greenhouse has easy access through the front, back and top, and its size and portability make it most useful. It will provide many years of service at minimal cost.

R. G. Hatfield
St. Paul, Nebraska

Greenhouses don't need to be complicated—they just need to be built securely and suit your needs. This one is gorgeous, and handy, too!

From the NHGC Staff...

What's a Biennial?

In horticultural terms, a biennial flower is one that must be planted in late summer or fall and then undergo a period of cold before it will bloom. For true biennials, the cold period is necessary to trigger the production of hormones within the plant which signal it to produce flowers. Foxglove (*Digitalis purpurea*) is a true biennial. If you plant it in spring, it will not flower until the following year. Many hardy annuals (and short-lived perennials such as sweet William and pansy) are grown as biennials, and are sometimes called winter annuals. Don't worry about all these words, but do remember that when trying any true biennial, you must start new plants in late summer or fall.

Chapter 6
Composting and Mulching Ideas

Good soil is the basis for a good garden. If your plants are growing in a soil they don't like, they'll never live up to their full potential. Luckily, even if you have horrible soil, you can improve it by adding compost and other kinds of vegetative matter. Here, our members hand down their composting, mulching and soil secrets for you. So if you're just starting out with a new bed or have one that's long established, you can get more from your plants than ever before.

GARDEN TALK

Compost Paper

Looking for an inexpensive source of organic matter to add to your compost pile? I know of one — the bags of shredded paper that banks and other businesses throw away. They make excellent compost or mulches. If you use them on your compost pile, be sure to add a little bit of fertilizer to help feed the organisms that help to break it down.

Phyllis Wilbur
Norfolk, Arkansas

A Natural Weed Barrier

If you lay several layers of newspaper down and cover the layers with wood chips, you'll have a great biodegradable mulch that will save you watering and weeding chores and expenses. Be sure to add a little bit of fertilizer to your plants, though, because the wood chips use nitrogen as they degrade. Sometimes they can take nitrogen away from your plants.

Marlys Eells
Isanti,
Minnesota

Newspaper makes a great weed barrier, but remember that it only lasts for about a season.

Collect Leaves

I recycle all my old plastic shopping bags by filling them full of leaves in autumn. Then I loosely fill the larger leaf bags with these. Staple the bags shut and use them to cover your tender plants in the winter. They help insulate against the cold. In the spring you can take the leaves out of the bags and add them to your compost pile. Save the bags for use next year since plastic won't rot.

Alice McConnell
Ely, Minnesota

Diaper Pails

I use old diaper pails I buy inexpensively from garage sales to store and carry my compost in. They look really pretty and the lids close tightly when you're not piling compost in them. They're easy and simple—with no smelly mess!

Cookie Bush
Pasadena, Maryland

From the NHGC Staff...

Landscape Fabric and Landscape Mesh

Landscaping companies often use landscape fabric to control weeds and erosion. It is rolled over the prepared ground before planting, and holes are cut to make places for plants. It is best used on slopes that are being planted with permanent shrubs. Because it does not decay, landscape fabric prevents spreading groundcovers from sending out runners and filling in. You must also use a straw or pine needle mulch over landscaping fabric; bark quickly washes away from a slick surface. When soil gets on top of landscaping fabric, weeds will manage to gain a foothold.

The best choice for holding soil while spreading groundcover plants become established is called landscape mesh. The mesh holds soil and young plants but allows plants to spread through the loose weave. It also breaks down approximately two years after being installed; by this time most groundcovers are fully mature and able to keep a bank from eroding.

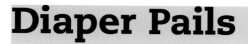

Know how far your plants will spread, then space them the correct distance apart so they'll fill in the gaps.

Hemp netting will hold the soil in place until these strawberries grow together into a groundcover.

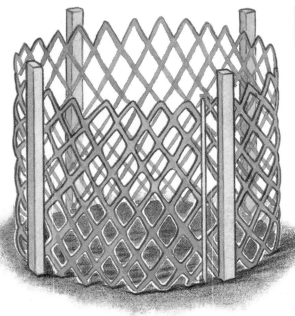

An Inexpensive Compost Pile

I build compost piles in my garden out of old plastic snow fencing. What I do is stand the fencing in one place and insert four to six stakes around it on lightweight fenceposts.

Then I start layering compost materials in the bin I've made. After a year or so of composting, I just remove the fencing and smooth out the compost over the garden. Then I start my pile over in another area of my garden.

Teri Caddle
Clayton, Illinois

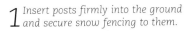

1 *Insert posts firmly into the ground and secure snow fencing to them.*

2 *Start adding your compost materials. It works well to layer—a layer of soil beneath a layer of vegetable matter, and so forth.*

3 *Once your compost is ready, use it in the garden.*

Wood chips make great mulch. You can sometimes get them from tree care specialists, or other sources.

Let Your Community Do the Work

Check your local recycling center. Ours produces large piles of free wood chips that I make into paths in our garden. They also have large piles of compost from recycled garden clippings and leaves. I can grow the best garden with only the effort of transporting these materials.

Ruth Meyers
Milford, New Hampshire

Quick Compost

I bought an old blender at a garage sale and use it to make "quick compost." I put coffee grounds, coffee filters and other vegetable kitchen scraps in it with some water. All you have to do is pour the mix in your compost pile or bury it in the garden. It's the best thing!

Carrie Soderstrom
Rhame, North Dakota

Cover Cropping

Be sure to dig your annual cover crop into the soil before it goes to seed—otherwise you'll have weeds!

Here's a trick to add fertility to your soil in the winter—use a cover crop. In the fall, plant your crop (oats or wheat or rye) in strips where you want garden rows next year. (I've found a garden seeder is very useful for this.) Put mulch in between these strips where you're going to walk. Then in spring, till under the green strips and plant your seed. As the green strips decompose, they add nutrients to the soil. You can mulch the ground after your seeds come up, to help preserve moisture. The next year, alternate the rows and plant your cover crop where you used to have the mulch paths.

Sophia Cameron
Hartley, Delaware

Add Some Kick to Your Climbing Roses

I sprinkle my morning coffee grounds around the base of my climbing roses. The coffee grounds add organic matter and nutrients to the soil as they decompose. My roses just love it!

Patricia Crowe
Princeton, Kentucky

Here's News

If you decide you want a new flower bed next spring, just cover the area with a layer of newspaper three to four pages thick. Then cover the top with black dirt. Over the winter, the paper will kill the grass and enrich the soil as it biodegrades. All you have to do is loosen the soil and start planting!

Judy Alward
Hudsonville, Michigan

Weed Barriers

I use large scraps of natural cloth (cotton, wool, that sort of thing) from my quilting and use them as weed barriers. You can't see them under the mulch and they're much cheaper than landscaping fabric. In time, they break down and add to the soil, so you get two benefits for the price of one!

Midge Price
Olympia, Washington

Advice *from the* Editor

Keeping Compost Clean

Never throw anything into your compost pile that you've sprayed herbicides on. These substances can stay potent in your compost—and cause problems for you later on when you use the compost you've created.

It's a good idea not to compost any weeds with seed heads— these seeds can stay alive in the compost and sprout when you plant them.

You can use nearly any kind of weed barrier you'd like—just be sure to cover it with mulch.

For the Birds; for the Flowers

I like to save all the ground corncob litter from the bottom of bird cages. Then I pour it outside on all my flower beds. It's a good, natural fertilizer, and my plants seem to just love it!

Mary Ann Biggs
Clio, Michigan

Cedar Mulch

I have a great mulching tip—use the cedar bedding for small animals. It really helps keeps down weeds, it smells great, and it repels insects. I freshen mine every year-and-a-half. (Don't ever use it for your vegetable garden, though, because it could spread diseases.)

Karen Johnson
Bay Saint Louis, Missouri

Make sure there is no pet waste in your cedar bedding—the waste can spread disease to humans.

From the NHGC Staff...

Compost—What Doesn't Go In

Material	Problem
Meat scraps, bones or fat	Attracts rodents and other pests.
Diseased plant debris	Can spread garden diseases.
Pesticide-treated plants or wood	May kill beneficial organisms.
Noxious weeds or weeds that have set seed	Can spread into garden.
Charcoal ashes	Much too alkaline.
Pet droppings	Often contain parasites.

Roses and Bananas

Chop up your banana peels and dig them into the ground around your roses. I have the most beautiful roses in my neighborhood thanks to my bananas.

Candy Dolan
Huntington Beach, California

Slugs Don't Like Eggs

Instead of throwing out your eggshells, crush them out and lay them on the soil. They'll help deter slugs, and they also add nutrients to the soil.

Jennifer Hess
Conover,
North Carolina

Save Your Grass

Lawn clippings work really well on the garden. They serve as a great mulch that keeps the weeds down; they keep disease down too, especially on tomatoes. That means there are fewer incidences of leaf spotting. As the grass breaks down it also serves as a natural fertilizer.

Amber Morrow
Maplewood, Minnesota

Raised Beds

If you build a raised bed, it only needs to be about a foot tall, but you can make it taller if you like. Lay a layer of compost over the spot where you'd like your bed. Then build your sides around the layer. Your plants will grow happily.

Rhonda Miller
Scottsburg, Indiana

Raised beds have many advantages: Water drains better; the soil warms up in spring; and weeding is easier because you don't have to bend over as far.

From the NHGC Staff...

Mulching Materials

As you select mulching materials, consider where they will be used. Ornamental plantings look best when mulched with attractive materials such as chopped bark or pine needles. Vegetable gardeners often use newspaper or straw.

Material	Primary Benefit	When and How to Apply
Lawn clippings	Builds soil structure. Moderates soil temperature. Conserves moisture.	Allow clippings to dry before applying. Apply a 1- to 4-inch layer that doesn't form a dense mat.
Chopped leaves	Suppresses weeds. Builds soil structure. Reduces soil temperature.	Chop or compost before using because whole leaves mat down. Mulch in winter or spring with a 3-inch layer.
Pine needles	Builds soil structure. Suppresses weeds. Increases acidity, good for acid-loving plants.	Apply a 2- to 4-inch layer around shrubs and trees. Pine needles tend to acidify the soil.
Bark nuggets	Conserves moisture. Suppresses weeds.	Apply a 2- to 3-inch layer around shrubs and trees, preferably over a roll-out mulch.
Straw or hay	Builds soil structure. Suppresses weeds. Moderates soil temperature. Conserves moisture.	Apply a 6-inch layer at planting time and as needed through the growing season. Straw usually contains fewer weed seeds than hay.

Roll-Out Mulches

Material	Primary Benefit	When and How to Apply
Paper, newspaper	Suppresses weeds. Conserves moisture.	Use between vining vegetables or in pathways between beds or rows. Cover with a thin layer of more attractive mulch. Turn under when partially decomposed.
Plastic weed barrier	Suppresses weeds. Conserves moisture.	Use beneath straw or grass clippings in places that are renovated at the end of the season. Reusable.
Plastic sheeting	Black plastic warms the soil and suppresses weeds. The light reflective patterns that accompany red plastic mulch benefits tomatoes and some other crops, and deters nematodes.	Lay down plastic and anchor with rocks or soil at planting time. Can also be laid down to warm the soil so you can plant earlier in spring than you normally would. Use heavyweight reusable products.
Landscape fabric	Suppresses weeds.	Lay down at planting time and cut slits for plants. Can be difficult to cut and doesn't allow plants to spread beyond the cut hole.

Chapter 7

Great Garden Design Ideas

Want to add something to your garden or yard but don't know where to start? This chapter is a great place to look. It's packed with ideas about the best plants to put together, elements to add to your garden, and plenty of other tips. When designing your garden, keep in mind that there are no real rules—only that you can do what you like! While you might not use every idea presented here, we're sure there's something for everyone.

Rocks have a natural beauty all their own. If brighter colors suit your style, though, go ahead and decorate your rocks!

More Than Rocks

I have a way to beautify my gardens with rocks we dig up from the garden. With acrylic paints, you can make colorful designs and customize them by putting favorite sayings from poems, songs, or the names of family members. It adds color and takes care of the rocks so you don't have to go through the work of getting rid of them.

Stephen & Darlene Modory
Barberton, Ohio

Perfect Pathways

I salvage old wooden planks. If you lay them on the ground, they make great rows through they garden, and don't get muddy. They help distribute your weight, too, so you don't compact the soil as much.

Winifred Waugh
Aurora, Colorado

If you don't like the look of a wooden plank, as shown here, you might consider mulching the area to cover it.

Tiered Waterfall Solves Shady Problem

We used to have a dead area in our front yard that I could never successfully grow anything in. It is heavily shaded by large maples which kept light away from new plants. I decided to give up the fight and fill the bare corner with a waterfall project.

My husband and I made three lily pad-shaped pools from ready-mix cement. To do this, we molded forms in a sand pile and then poured cement into them. We let them cure for one week and then waterproofed them with concrete waterproofing sealer. We positioned them so that the largest pad with two spouts sits over the two smaller pads. This way, water trickles down three tiers and into the recycle pond we built into the base. We also installed a small pond pump to circulate the water.

Now the sound of the falling water can be very soothing while I'm sitting or working outside. I put a variety of artificial plants around the pond to add some green foliage and color. Ken helped wire in several spotlights so that we could enjoy the lily pond at night. We have received many compliments from passers-by, but the best part was being able to work on this project together.

Joy and Ken Mott
Sandpoint, Idaho

Water features don't only belong outside—many gardeners are using them in their homes and on their patios, too.

GARDEN TALK

Advice *from the* Editor

Size Does Matter

It always helps to know how big a plant will grow before you plant it. Shrubs won't do well if they're planted too close to a house, for instance, and a mighty 80-foot tree will look out of place in an average small city lot.

Natural Steppingstones

If you have quite a few flat stones in your yard that you don't know what to do with, I have a suggestion: Make a great-looking pathway that you can even mow over. How? By burying stones in the ground just below ground level. Leave some grass to grow between the stones and you have a fashionable pathway.

Lynn Marion
North Bend, Washington

Have an Extra Bowling Ball?

Instead of using rocks to decorate my garden, I recycle old bowling balls. They add much-needed color during the winter months and have a pleasing, unusual look. I've had many passers-by stop to look at my garden ornaments. (Tell children that they're not plastic balls, though — it could hurt if the kids tried to kick them around.)

*Glenda Smith
Buckley,
Washington*

Here's a perfect example of stretching the garden imagination, and having fun. Bowling balls as garden decor? They're colorful, interesting, free ... why not?

For More Hanging Baskets

If you have lots of extra metal coat hangers around but can't find a use for them, try this. Start by uncoiling them. Then wrap one end around a tree branch and tie it off so that it's secure. Then bend the other end up to make a loop and wrap it around itself. You can hang hanging baskets from here to add more color to your garden, especially to places where you can't grow other plants.

John Jessmore
Elmira, New York

Hanging baskets have a special charm—and you can plant them with almost all your favorite plants.

Plants to Plant Together

I love to plant feverfew, red climbing roses (*Rosa* spp.), monkshood (*Aconitum* spp.), magenta petunias (*Petunia* spp.), deep blue lobelia (*Lobelia erinus*) and dusty miller (*Senecio cineraria*) together to keep color in my garden all season long.

Jill Jorgenson
Washington Island, Wisconsin

Feverfew.

Color contrasts add life to the garden. Here pink, purple and silver make a beautiful statement.

Advice *from the* Editor

Texture Is Important, Too

Consider the leaves as well as the flowers when you plant perennials. Fine-leafed plants, such as astilbe, contrast very well with bolder-leafed plants, for example hostas. When your plants quit blooming, the foliage contrast will still be attractive.

Annual Success

In the fall, take cuttings of your coleus, impatiens or other easily rooted annuals and bring them indoors. Grow them as houseplants through the winter. Then in the spring, after your tulips and daffodils are done blooming, you can plant the annuals outside to hide the fading foliage. In about a month they fill in all of the empty spaces and you don't waste any valuable garden spots.

Jill Jorgenson
Washington Island, Wisconsin

Bishop's weed (Aegopodium) has a fine texture—especially the variegated type.

Keeping Track

Make a garden journal. Take an old notebook and scrap paper and take notes on expenses, catalogs you ordered from, what seeds produced well and which didn't, and other things you would find useful. It helps you learn from your mistakes. If you refer to it each year, you can fine-tune your gardening process.

Clare Hafferman
Kalispell, Montana

Gazebo Has Family Waiting in Line to Relax

My husband, Bob, designed and built this unique corner gazebo in our backyard. The gazebo, which was built with redwood, has a shake shingle roof. Bob had particular fun hanging onto the roof so as to not fall while he was shingling it. The inside ceiling is lined with cedar strips, which not only look great but smell great, too. Bob also attached a fan to the center of the ceiling, which was a little tricky because of the pitch. The fan looks and works great, especially on those hot summer days in Arizona.

Bob also installed fluorescent lights around the outer edge of the gazebo. These fixtures light both the inside and outside, providing a pleasant place to sit at night. To give us the final relaxing touch, he hung a set of speakers running off of our radio and CD player in the house. Now we can enjoy our favorite music in the backyard.

We all just love this gazebo—our daughters, grandkids, family and friends. Sometimes you even have to wait to get an open chair. Bob has given us a great place to enjoy the outdoors, right here at home. I'm a very proud wife.

Ellen and Bob Frisby
Glendale, Arizona

The Powells' slope is in the background of the photo.

King of the Hill

Our yard has a severe slope in the back—a 20-foot drop that started about 10 feet from the foundation and went down and out about 38 feet. To help make the slope useable, we planted different ornamental grasses for easy maintenance. They look good, too!

The Powells
Kent, Washington

Inexpensive Paths

I made a pathway through my shade garden. I used a bag of cement mix to make blocks of stone (mine are about 22 inches across). I put all the individual stones together to make a beautiful path that's much less expensive than buying expensive flagstones or paving stones.

Joy Owens
Overland Park, Kansas

A "Stream Side" Garden

If you have a hill in your yard or even a berm, you can take advantage of it for a special project. On top of the hill, take an old maple bucket or whiskey barrel and plant flowers in it. Then make a "stream" running down from it out of small, white stones (or even river stones) with a flower planted here or there on the edges to help make it look natural. It's a great addition that's a lot of fun.

Ruth Ramsey
Hagerstown,
Maryland

Mini-Beds

Here's a tip to keep in mind next time you want to add a new garden bed—make mini-beds. They have easy access for you and require minimal weeding. To make them, first lay out your outside border and then free-form mini-beds inside of it. Line your mini-beds with rocks, landscape timbers or bricks. Leave enough room between your beds for paths so you can walk and bend down to work. Then lay landscaping fabric or black plastic along all the open spaces between your mini-beds, to make pathways. Mulch over the top and you don't have to worry anymore.

Susan Carter
Richmond, Ohio

You don't need water to make a lovely "stream." Try creating a river of stones!

Keep a Log

If you sometimes forget what plants you ordered between January when the catalogs come out and May when the companies ship your orders, keep the information in a three-ring binder. I fill out my order form and then phone in my order. I write which credit card I use on the form, as well as the person I spoke to, the date, and the order number they give me. I also glue a picture and description from the catalog on a blank sheet of paper and put this with the order sheet. At the end of the season, I make notes about whether or not the plants did well, tasted good, or other things that I might want to remember next year when I order. I'm always improving my garden that way!

Leslie O'Keefe
Foster City, California

Add a Garden

There used to be a swimming pool in our backyard. Since we never used it anymore, we decided to have it removed. After the concrete was gone (a big job), we filled the area in with soil and then planted grass on top. (You could plant flowers, too, if you want.) It's a lot less work and we enjoy it so much more. It's especially nice if you have a smallish yard because then you can have more space.

Dianne Cook
Hickory,
North Carolina

Free Edging May be Worth the Work

Ever wonder how to edge flower beds? I have a great way! Just recycle old concrete by taking broken pieces from ruined driveways or sidewalks when they're being replaced. Use the pieces for edging your flower beds or making pathways through your garden. I've never found anyone who isn't willing to let me haul off their concrete chunks for them for free!

Leah Hamilton
Yuma, Arizona

Add a Pond

I made a pond in my backyard. Using a garden hose, I outlined the shape of the pond that I wanted. After that, I dug the area out, making it anywhere from 4 to 18 inches deep. (I wanted my pond to have two levels.) Then I used some cement to form the bottom of the pool. Make sure you use the right kind—some cements are very porous. I used the hose again to lay out the shape of the flower beds I wanted all around the pond and dug out the sod. I edged the bed with rocks and mulched it. It's beautiful!

Pamela Ward
Winfield, Missouri

Soften the Look of Chainlink

Finely textured plants such as this coreopsis (Coreopsis verticillata) are especially good at softening the look of chainlink.

To make the work of cutting weeds and pulling grass out of the bottom of a chainlink fence much easier, I plant groundcovers like ajuga or daylilies at the base of the fence. Both of these groundcovers (as well as many others) grow thick enough to smother any weeds and grass, plus they look great!

Teri Caddle
Clayton, Illinois

Hanging Herbs

I recently bought a house that had mature landscaping all around it. It was very nice, but this left me with little space for an herb garden like I dreamed about. I really wanted one so I had to get creative. What I did was purchase a couple of shepherd's poles and then planted all of my herbs in hanging baskets. It gave me lots of room for all kinds of herbs, and I don't have to bend down to harvest or care for them.

Pat Chandler
Houston, Texas

Terraces add depth and dimension to a flat yard.

It Works on Many Levels

Wondering how you can add extra depth and dimension to your yard? I found that I could—all I had to do was add some terraces. Even if it's a flat yard, you can add height or depth by digging terraces down and adding them up.

Sue Solomon
Dallas, Texas

Garden Ornaments

Do you get really mad when you end up breaking a terra-cotta pot? Instead of throwing it away, you can be happy by recycling it. That way, you can keep all of your old, broken pots. "Plant" them next to your tomato and other plants. When you go to water, fill these old pots and let the water slowly seep out for your plants' roots. You can also do this with old coffee cans with holes punched in the bottoms or other kinds of containers where the water will slowly go out.

Laura Taylor
Woodlake, California

Add a Surprise or Two

I had an old strawberry pot that cracked during the winter. I hated to just throw it out, so I placed pieces of it out in my garden to look like an archaeological find. In spring, daffodils pop up around the pieces, and in summer, sedum creeps around and through the shards. It's a lot more fun now!

Claire Tremblay
Westport, Massachusetts

Let Your Houseplants Take a Vacation

Do you have a shady spot in your yard that you're not sure what to do with? Try planting houseplants outside in those shady spots. They'll grow bigger than you might think they can. Everyone will be amazed at how big the plants will grow and what they look like.

Cathy Streeter
De Kalb Junction, New York

Houseplants that are especially good for outside use include philodendrons, pothos and dieffenbachia.

Color Combinations

I grow a mound of blue irises with columbines in the same shade of blue. The big irises really highlight the dainty columbine. It's really striking to have different plants that bloom in the same hues. A number of plants come in the same color and bloom at the same time.

Barbara Shepard
Fort Wayne, Indiana

Plant Angel's Trumpet with Glads

I have a beautiful wide-spreading datura. Since the flowers only open at night, I wanted more color. That's when I thought to plant my giant mixed gladiolus around it. They grew up through the datura's branches and bloom above it during the day, while its branches help support them and stop them from blowing over in the wind.

Lynn McLane
Shelby,
Alabama

From the NHGC Staff...

When Flowers Wear White

There are plenty of good things to say about white flowers. They never cause clashes and they glow in moonlight or partial shade. White tends to make small spaces seem larger and more spacious. On the down side, white is simply not very exciting. Since many white flowers turn brown as they fade, it helps to choose white flowers that clean themselves, such as impatiens, nierembergia, nicotiana and pansies.

Plant spikey glads with spreading angel's trumpet to add wonderful contrast to your garden.

Remember that in your garden, whatever you like goes!

Ambitious Fence Building

I decided to construct a fence around my property for the sake of my pet German shepherd, my privacy and my serenity. In one week and with plenty of sunshine, I built 155 feet of 6-foot-tall fencing. It is custom-designed with two sets of large gates so I can drive in and store a travel trailer during the winter. I'm 52 years old, and had knee replacement surgery before building the fence, so building it was quite an undertaking.

I dug all the post holes, poured my own concrete footings, set and leveled the posts, hung the 2 x 4 rails and screwed in more than 200 fence boards. The whole fence is made of cedar. I also hand-built my own lattice from strips of lath. Then I stained the fence driftwood gray.

I built a smaller version of the fence using leftover lumber to surround my flower garden along the house. Surplus concrete from other projects helped me create a water fountain next to the fence. I've planted flowers to help conceal the concrete.

Since I own only basic tools, I built the fence with a circular saw, shovel and drill. I'm very proud of the results.

Joyce Verhaag
Spokane, Washington

This great fence adds both beauty and privacy.

Successful Dry Streambeds

If you'd like to add interest to your yard and garden, consider adding a dry streambed. Just lay out a water hose in the shape you think a stream would flow through your yard. Then remove all of the grass, then dig a trench where the stream will be. Line the trench with plastic or landscaping fabric and fill it with rocks. It helps to place the rocks so they look natural—bigger ones toward the edges and little ones in the middle. Along areas of the side, plant flowers.

Tommie Young
Bradford, Pennsylvania

Your Favorite Photo Album

Want to make your spring bulb displays look even better? Just take some photos of them every couple of weeks when they're blooming. By the time you can plant new spring bulbs, all of yours have faded into the ground. If you have your photos to refer to, you can fill in any spaces that you might not remember anymore.

Maryann Kinsella Lakewood, New Jersey

Take photos of your bulb beds when they're in full bloom. Then you'll know exactly where to fill in when it's time to add more bulbs.

GARDEN TALK

Hydrangeas belong in nearly every garden.

Don't Waste Space

Don't forget about your side yards when planting! In ours, we put dwarf Canadian hemlock, impatiens, hydrangea and other wonderful plants.

Cindy Beck
Du Bois, Pennsylvania

Biennial Success

If you plant foxgloves or other biennials, plant some seed each year. Because they don't bloom the first year, you'll have blooms every year after that, especially if you let them reseed.

Beatrice Daniel
Henderson, North Carolina

From the NHGC Staff...

Companionable Combinations

Many of the best annual and perennial cut flowers grow quite tall, which is an important consideration when growing them interspersed with bulbs and tubers. The latter may be grown as clumps or drifts in a mixed border or you can use them in combination with low-growing plants such as dwarf annuals and groundcovers. Here are 10 planting schemes that work especially well with bulbs, corms and tubers.

- Set out tulips in the fall, overplanted with a single color of pansy.
- Plant daffodils or tulips where forget-me-nots have naturalized into a thick edging or groundcover.
- On a sunny slope, make a permanent partnership of large-flowered daffodils and creeping phlox or thrift.
- Plant a dozen bright blue alliums or vivid gladiolus in a round clump, and mass silver-gray artemisias around their base.
- Hide the heavy feet of bearded iris with a permanent groundcover of *Vinca minor*.

- Interplant daffodils with daylilies. The daylilies will hide the daffodil foliage when it is at its worst.
- Use petite johnny-jump-ups to mask the bases of lanky lilies.
- Plant early daffodils beneath deciduous trees that do not leaf out until late spring.
- Naturalize long-lived bulbs with blooming groundcover plants such as perennial candytuft (white) or ajuga (purple).
- Flank dahlias with short-lived spring annuals such as tassel flower or calendula, and pull out the annuals when the dahlias need more room to grow.

Color Contrasts

Want a design idea? Try mass plantings of pale or dark colors using bright colors as accents. It's very effective. A sea of light blue forget-me-nots, for example, with a few red tulips really guides your eye through the garden.

Kathy Niver
Hebron, Connecticut

Beautiful red celosia stands out against lavender Brazilian verbena.

A Great Combination

I plant my hostas with Virginia bluebells. The bluebells flower and look great in the early spring, but then die down by summer. The foliage of the hostas fills the gaps.

Kathy Niver
Hebron, Connecticut

Hostas make wonderful companions to plants that go dormant, such as old-fashioned bleeding heart.

Most clematis are climbers—don't be afraid to use shrubs as supports.

Lilacs provide wonderful spring color, but could use some dressing up later in the season. Flowering vines are just the solution.

Longer-Lasting Color

I plant my clematis on my lilacs. The lilacs help shade the clematis roots and the clematis adds color when the lilacs are done blooming. Most clematis aren't big enough to smother the lilacs.

Kathy Niver
Hebron, Connecticut

Something to Look At

Looking for a way to add some "zing" to your garden? I found that if you add a rare and interesting plant as a focal point, it really gets highlighted and shines—giving your garden a different feel. Some wonderful, interesting plants are weeping shrubs and variegated plants.

Amy Neigebauer
Owatonna, Minnesota

The Other Grass

Is mowing your turfgrass all the time a lot of work? Here's a way to lighten the load. Instead of planting your backyard in all grass, add a section of mixed wildflowers and ornamental grasses. It will decrease maintenance and add a splash of color to your yard.

Amy Neigebauer
Owatonna, Minnesota

Pond Pleasures

This pond project design is really two tiered ponds with a waterfall flowing between them. The lower pool features a small fountain and a pump to circulate water back up to the upper pool. I carefully laid a fieldstone border around the entire structure and added plenty of plants to give the pond a more natural appearance. It's great to relax in our swing and hear the sound of falling water in our backyard.

Gene P. Schell
Bartonville, Texas

Water features tend to lend themselves to a tropical look. Bananas seem perfectly in place.

Combine Colors

Bold color tones go well together—see how well the golden Dahlberg daisy blends with red and purple.

Looking for new plants to try together? One combination that I've found to be particularly striking is planting the dwarf morning glory 'Enchantment' (*Convolvulus tricolor*) with a yellow plant such as Dahlberg daisy or golden flax. What a beautiful color combination!

Amy Neigebauer
Owatonna, Minnesota

From the NHGC Staff...

A Garden for Everyone

Permanent beds. *Working within defined activity areas makes the garden more beautiful, and the rotation and planting possibilities increase.*

Ornament. *In the center, where the paths cross, we might find a sundial, birdbath, or a favorite garden ornament.*

Edible flowers. *In a kitchen garden, plants like gem marigolds and nasturtiums serve the dual purpose of beauty and food production.*

Herbs. *A large variety of flowers and herbs could be interplanted or could edge the main beds.*

Fragrant and cutting flowers. *When space is limited, concentrate on special favorites of the gardeners.*

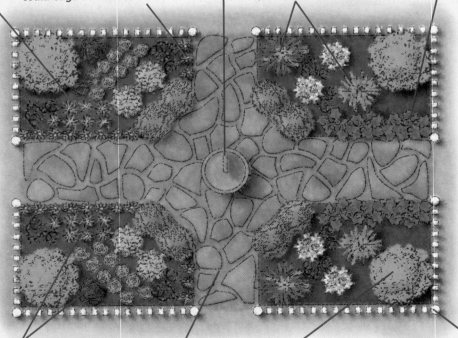

Salad vegetables. *In this size garden it may make sense to concentrate on growing primarily those things you want to cook with but simply can't buy locally.*

Hard surface path. *For low maintenance and a more passive form of involvement, a brick or stone path promotes easy, mud-free access to the beds.*

Fruit bushes. *In the four corners might be blueberries or even trellis-trained currants or gooseberries for visual impact and to make special preserves for Christmas gifts.*

Enclosure. *A partly porous fence, such as a picket fence or lattice, allows just enough air through to still air currents while blocking the major force of the wind.*

River-Rock Walls Increase Curb Appeal

We built two rock walls, and put boxwood plants between the walls, with red rock on the bottom next to the street. We moved the top plants around, and put in a sprinkler system. We also put rock around the birch tree on the left.

The rocks for the wall are river rocks from the Columbia River. My wife and I made many trips to the river.

Greg and Jamie Englert
Vancouver, Washington

Sometimes landscaping just looks "okay."

Here's what the same home can look like after some extra time and attention.

From the NHGC Staff...

Landscaping with Shrubs

Adopting any shrub requires careful thought and planning, for these plants are likely to be with you for many years. The best cultivars also tend to be quite expensive. Of course you want your shrubs to yield attractive cut material, but the right shrub planted in the right place can do much more. In addition to their most common job of masking the foundation of your house, shrubs can be used to screen out unwanted views or frame more desirable ones. Those with prickles or thorns can be used to deter intruders, and hedges or narrow thickets can define boundaries. You also can use shrubs to accent entryways, hide utility equipment or anchor visual focal points such as statuary or a water garden.

For cutting purposes, the most desirable shrubs have much to offer beyond a blob of green color. They may produce showy flowers (azaleas), not-so-showy flowers followed by pretty berries (beautyberry), or an irresistible combination of fragrant flowers, followed by colorful berries, followed by vivid fall foliage (viburnums). Shrubs that produce berries usually attract birds or squirrels, which provide yet another avenue of garden enjoyment.

Chapter 8
Container Plants—Inside and Out

There's a place for containers in every garden—a houseplant in a sunny window, a terra-cotta pot on an apartment balcony, an accent near your front door. With containers there's almost no limit to what you can do! They allow you to mix soils to suit certain plants, and they come in a wide variety of forms, colors and textures. While container gardening is usually fairly easy, this chapter has ideas that should make it even easier.

A New, Old Workspace

Ever make a mess when you're repotting? I've found that an old cookie sheet (one you don't use for baking) serves as a great working surface when repotting plants. If you spill soil, it just lands on the sheet instead of making a mess. The sheet also works as a tray to hold potted plants so when you water you don't have to have saucers underneath each pot to stop the water.

June Garcia
Honokaa, Hawaii

Be Creative with Pots!

Look for old items to recycle and add decoration to your garden. I find old, hollow logs to make planters from; I have an old cast-iron sink with flowers in it and I have two antique soap kettles that I propped on their sides and planted annuals in. They look so nice in the garden when you plant in them!

Helen Cole
Wichita, Kansas

Don't be afraid to be creative—your garden is supposed to reflect your personality.

Saving Water

I save rainwater for all my potted plants. To do this, just adjust the downspout on your house or garage so that it runs into a big 35-gallon drum. It's better for your plants than a lot of tapwater (which often has chemicals, such as chlorine, added). Plus, you can save money on your water bill (or your energy bill if you have a well and need to pump water).

Terri Hobbs
North Pole,
Alaska

Let Your Plants Do the Work

If you need to be away from your potted plants and are worried about them not getting enough moisture, soak a cotton shoelace in water and cut the plastic ends off. Push one end of the shoelace into the soil deep enough so that it's near the plant's roots. Leave the other end in a bucket of water. The moisture will travel through the cotton right to the plant. That way, the plant gets just the right amount of water it needs.

Debbie Ingold
Peoria, Illinois

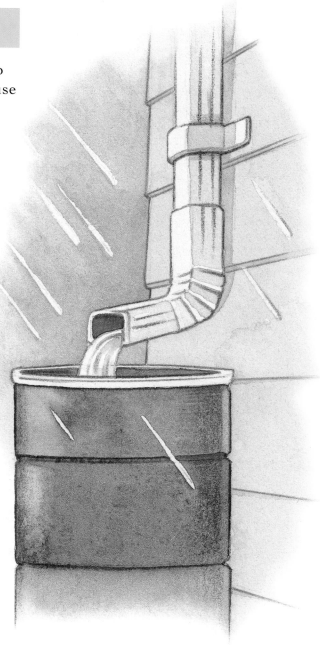

Utilize rainwater. It's free, and good for your plants.

GARDEN TALK

Advice *from the* Editor

Pick the Right Container

Make sure that any containers you plant your plants in have drainage holes. If water isn't allowed to escape, the roots rot and the plant can die. If excess water drains away, there's less chance that your plants will get too much water.

Recycle Your Coffee Filters

I heard that placing pottery shards in the bottom of your containers doesn't help them drain better. So to keep the soil from running out the holes on the bottom, I had to figure something else out. I realized that I can place coffee filters in the bottoms of my pots. This helps keep the soil from washing out, and still lets water drain. (Plus you keep insects out, too.)

Monica Bengston
Independence, Iowa

Decorating with Devil's Ivy

I decorate the inside of my house with devil's ivy. It is one of the easiest to care for and quickest-growing houseplants. It can frame doorways and windows. If you have two hanging pots, you can grow the plant into a living arch. I have some making a headboard for my bed. That way, I get to wake up to the sight of living greenery. What more could you ask for!

Jill McMahan
Indianapolis, Indiana

CONTAINERS

Keep Bugs Out

I use old canvas to cover the inside of the bottoms of my potted plants. All you need to do is set your pot on a piece of canvas, trace the size of the bottom of the pot, then cut the tracing out. It fits right inside the pot and stops the soil from draining out or pests from getting in.

Marguerite Jandreau
Augusta, Maine

To keep your potted plants happy, make sure they're watered well and have good drainage.

No Perlite Allowed!

Amaryllis and other plants related to lilies, like Easter lilies, clivias and agapanthus, do best in a soil media mixture that does not include perlite (the white balls of rock that look like Styrofoam). Perlite may leach a chemical into the soil and plants such as amaryllis may get leaf burn from that chemical.

Amber Morrow Maplewood, Minnesota

Once your clivia blooms, try using it as a cut flower and then enjoy the plant for its foliage.

To keep your pebbles from mixing into the soil, try using a cover—such as a piece of weed barrier with holes cut in for the plants—between the stone and soil.

Stop Splashing

I have a tip for happier window boxes in the spring and summer before the plants completely fill out. All you need to do is put a small layer of decorative gravel on top of the soil in your window boxes. It improves the appearance while the plants are young (hides the soil) and also keeps your window from being splashed with mud when it rains or when you water.

Doris Yoder
Manton, Michigan

Pinecone Solution

I line the bottom of my window boxes with pinecones. The space at the bottom allows for better drainage. Plus, at the end of the season, when you dump your window box soil into your compost pile, you don't have to spend time picking out the pinecones like you would Styrofoam peanuts or rocks.

Amy Peterson
Minneapolis, Minnesota

The Bottom Layer

To recycle old pop cans and bottles, place a layer of them in the bottom of your large planting containers. It will make them much lighter so you can move them around if you need to, and it will also help the container's drainage because the water flows to the bottom and doesn't leave the soil saturated.

Vyki Hannappel
Newport,
North Carolina

Clay pots drain more quickly than their plastic counterparts because the clay has tiny pores that water can escape from.

Lighten Your Pots

I put those Styrofoam chunks that come in mail-order packages in the bottom of my pots. They help encourage drainage and you recycle them at the same time. It also makes the pots lighter. (If you do this, make sure you don't use the biodegradable kind—otherwise they'll all melt the first time you water.)

Sally Haider
Lacey,
Washington

GARDEN TALK

Use Barrels

Planting in old barrels makes gardening a lot easier. There's no need to bend over as far, and that makes weeding a lot less of a chore. (And who wouldn't mind that?) It looks more interesting if you prop the barrels up on different levels, too.

Mildred Tyler
Lucerne Valley, California

Here's How to Get the Most Out of Rain

To collect more natural rainwater, try installing a plastic gutter system to both sides of your house, garage or shed. It's easy if you attach a pipe spout with a shutoff arm to the ends of two 55 gallon barrels. Turn the barrels on their sides, lay them on frames and strap them on into place. Cut a hole, opposite of the spout end, to accommodate the downspout from the building. Make sure the downspout side is higher than the end with the shutoff arm.

Linda Goerdt
Hibbing, Minnesota

Advice *from the* Editor

Help Those Houseplants

If you'd like to add humidity to the air around your houseplants, but don't like the look of a tray of pebbles or sand, try using a saucer larger than your pot. Place your plant with its saucer into the larger one and fill the larger one with water. As long as you don't fill it up too much, your saucer will keep the bottom of your pot dry, and still let water drain away from your plant. The water in the large saucer will evaporate to give you the humidity.

Your Houseplants Will Love You for It

I collect rainwater for all my houseplants. You never know what they add to tap water and it could be too alkaline for your plants.

Richard Thompson
Bolingbrook, Illinois

Make Your Own Planter

I made a wonderful planter out of a 6-inch piece of PVC pipe with 2-inch holes. I filled it with soil and planted it like a strawberry jar, using fibrous begonias. They filled in so thickly that you couldn't see the PVC pipe by the end of the season. It looked like a tower of begonias!

Jean Haverstock
Dayton, Ohio

While this ingenious PVC pipe plant stand might not look the best early on, it will be an absolute showstopper later.

GARDEN TALK

Don't Let It Escape!

Plant your Missouri primrose (*Oenothera macrocarpa*) in containers. If you don't, it could spread all over and take over your garden.

Kristie Weinkauf
Jasper, Minnesota

Wonderful Houseplants

I take cuttings of my impatiens and save them every year so I don't have to continually buy new plants each year. It saves me a lot of money and gives me color in the house during the winter.

Dawn Macrillo
Stratford, New Jersey

Impatiens are beautiful—inside and out.

Making Watering Less of a Chore

Do you have a lot of houseplants spread throughout your house? If so, you know what a chore watering can be. I learned that if I place containers of water throughout the house (behind sofas, chairs, curtains, or cupboards), there's always one close by my plants. It makes the process much easier and helps add humidity in the winter when your air is especially dry inside the house.

Roslyn Hancock
Pleasant Grove, Utah

Pretty Planters

You can use chimney flue tiles as raised planters. If you use different lengths, sizes and shapes, you can make a variety of configurations.

Gene Hall
Chester, Connecticut

Advice *from the* Editor

Like a Gentle Rain

It helps to place many types of houseplants in the shower and give them a nice "rain" periodically. The water from the shower will help clean off any dust that builds up on the leaves. This dust decreases the amount of light that your plants get, so they'll do much better when you clean them up. If you cover the soil with Saran-type plastic or another barrier, there's no mess to clean up.

Beautiful hydrangeas can be fussy.

Keep Your Hydrangeas Happy

Hydrangea plants (in pots) are very water sensitive. They tend to take up a lot of water—and if they wilt they don't recover very readily with just a watering. If you place the plant (after watering) in a plastic bag, it raises the humidity and acts as a greenhouse. Hydrangeas recover more quickly this way.

Amber Morrow
Maplewood, Minnesota

Successful Potting Benches

My husband made me a great potting bench out of an old screen door. I am able to dry plants on top of the screen and pot them over the solid part of the door. I use the screen part as a sift, too, to clean debris from my soil. It works wonderfully!

Lisa Steiner
Englewood, Colorado

Amaryllis in the Garden

Amaryllis, which is traditionally planted in the winter for winter blooming as a houseplant, will also do well if you plant it in the garden during the summer. Sometimes I've forgotten to plant or haven't had time to plant my amaryllis in the winter, so I then plant them in my garden and they bloom just fine there, too. Just don't forget to dig them up again in the fall if you live in an area where it freezes in winter.

Amber Morrow
Maplewood, Minnesota

From the NHGC Staff...

Terra-cotta

Made of inexpensive low-fired clay, terra-cotta pots have been loved by gardeners for thousands of years. Besides the simple unglazed terra-cotta, glazed terra-cotta in shining colors adds beauty to the garden and can be chosen to coordinate with flower bloom. Unglazed pots must be watered more often because the clay breathes and the pores allow moisture to escape, letting the potting mix dry out quicker. This is perfect for plants that like to dry out in between waterings, but less suitable for moisture-loving plants. Unglazed terra-cotta pots are also more susceptible to cold weather, often cracking and crumbling when they freeze. Of course, glazed terra-cotta will cost a bit more.

GARDEN TALK

All-Inclusive Garden Potting Bench

My wife spends as much free time as possible working in the yard. Potting plants is one of her greatest pleasures, so she asked me to build a potting bench to allow her to easily perform her favorite tasks. Knowing that she has a bad back required that everything be at or above waist height, to keep her bending to a minimum. Easy access to tools, containers, water and soil preparation materials was also a necessity.

Using these criteria, I began my design. I researched several books and magazines and found articles which contained portions of what I wanted, and I incorporated them into my own all-inclusive plan. The simple design I came up with can be altered to suit most needs dictated by any site.

The basic frame is made from redwood 2 x 4s. The four uprights are cut to 7 feet from standard 8-foot stock. Two rectangular top/shelf support boxes are constructed of 2 x 4s to fit inside the uprights and maintain the 6-foot x 27-inch overall bench dimension limits. One shelf support box is nailed in place about 6 inches from the ground to form the support for the inside lower storage shelf. The second top support box is nailed in place 3 feet from the ground to provide the support for the bench top. Once the upper 2 x 4 bench top support box is installed, a 6-foot x 27-inch piece of ¾-inch exterior plywood is cut and installed on the newly formed surface. Dado cuts are made in the four corners to accept the inset of the four uprights.

A 1 x 2 frame is placed around the perimeter of the plywood bench top, flush with the plywood top surface and overlapping the outside of the 2 x 4 uprights. This frame

The finished project boasts a tile potting surface, a wet sink with drainage, shelter from the sun, and ample ventilated storage enclosed by redwood lattice.

should be glued and nailed to the plywood edge. Near one end of the bench top a hole is cut in the plywood top for a plastic tub to be used as a sink.

Next, I installed 12-inch square tile on the bench top, then added a dark tobacco-colored grout after the tiles had set in the mortar base. The tile was allowed to set for a few days, then the plastic sink was fitted with a drain and an adapter to allow connection of a garden hose remnant. The sink was set into a perimeter bead of RTV caulking.

The front enclosure doors are made from a single 6-foot-long by 2½-foot-wide 1 x 2 frame. I stapled redwood lattice to the door-frame assembly in two sections. I also attached lattice to each end of the enclosed bench area, and to the back of the lower bench area, extending about a foot above the bench top. A 6-foot piece of 1 x 2 along the top edge of the 1-foot lattice overlap forms a trimmed edge.

Once this was done, I placed a 4 x 6-foot piece of lattice on a 1 x 2 frame mounted on top of the 7-foot vertical members to act as a sun-filtering shield above the potting bench. A 1 x 2 frame around the top lattice perimeter strengthens the lattice piece.

Finally, I ran a ½-inch water line connected at the closest water source to a faucet in the potting bench and extended the drain hose out to the garden area. I set the structure on bricks to prevent ground contact, then applied redwood sealer to all wood surfaces.

John J. Adams
Newbury Park, California

A faucet carries water supply from the house, and a drain hose connected to the sink leads to the garden.

A close-up detail of the drain hose and how the connection is made to the sink drain.

Chapter 9
Tool Tips

We all end up using gardening tools of one sort or another. Some of us end up using the regulars—hoes, shovels and rakes. Others get creative, though, and this chapter contains some of their best ideas. Using the right tool can make your job far easier than using the wrong tool—or none at all. Check out some of these ideas. They're sure to help make your efforts go much further the next time you're out in the garden.

Portable Toolshed

I have always wanted a toolshed, but don't have room for one. I improvised by buying a plastic garbage can on wheels. This is my shed. It allows me to store fertilizers, unused edging, hand tools and whatever I need—plus I get to wheel it around where I need it.

Cindy Elmore
St. Ann, Missouri

Try These Gloves on for Size

Are you tired of buying gardening gloves because the ones you have wear out? Here's a solution I came up with. I buy old-fashioned cotton dress gloves from garage sales (but you can use thin cotton work gloves if you want). Put them on, and wear a pair of disposable latex exam gloves on top. You can use the exam gloves several times before they rip and you keep your hands clean and dry while you work.

Theresa Petti
Nutley, New Jersey

Gloves are important gardening tools.

Tools for All

I am wheelchair bound, so it can be hard to use all my tools. To help make using them easier, I took my good, trusty hand trowel and taped a wooden handle to it. That way, I could use it better. It makes planting plants very easy. I also purchase children-sized garden tools with short handles to dig, rake and weed. I can still have all my gardens this way.

Sally Haider
Lacey,
Washington

Color Your Straws for Marking

Have trouble wondering where you planted bulbs after the foliage has dried up and gone dormant for the season? A solution is to stick old drinking straws in the ground to mark where you planted your spring-flowering bulbs. You can even color-coordinate the straws so you remember which marks what bulbs. (Color them yellow for daffodils or blue for grape hyacinths, for example.)

Susan Carter
Richmond, Ohio

Use colored floss on marker sticks to denote the bloom color on each of your spring-blooming plants. Come fall, should you decide to divide, you'll know which plant is which!

Mark the Colors

If you plan on dividing your tulips, iris or other spring-blooming plants in the fall, tie a small piece of embroidery floss around a marker (of any sort, even a chopstick!) next to the plant. The floss could match the color of the bloom, so then you know exactly what's planted there and you don't get confused. During the summer and fall, your garden guests won't even see the floss unless they're looking for it.

Geniel Johnson
Springfield, Missouri

Mailboxes in the Garden

For a great place to keep your tools close at hand so you won't lose any of them again, simply take an old mailbox and attach it to a fence in your yard. The tools won't get wet when it rains and you will always know where they are. Plus, it's easier to tell people where the tools are if you need someone to get something for you. You can even decorate the mailbox for a special, personalized touch, too. (Keep it shut when you're not using it, though; birds might choose to nest inside!)

Cathy Steiben
Naples, Maine

Add a Bumper to Your Trimmer

To extend the life of my lawn string trimmer, I've glued an appropriate-sized metal cap (a regular 1-inch-diameter nut or washer, for example) onto the "bump knob" that extends the line on the trimmer. I made this simple modification to protect the plastic knob on the trimmer from wear and tear caused by continual banging against the ground. I hope it will make my trimmer last forever!

I. Turman
Chicago, Illinois

A metal washer reinforces the plastic bump knob on this trimmer, extending the tool's life.

From the NHGC Staff...

Tools for Tree Pruning

Several tools make tree pruning easy. Use scissors-type pruners (1) on small stems and twigs. Long-handled loppers (2) give you good leverage on larger branches. Never force a lopper to cut through a branch that is too large or you will damage the plant.

A folding pruning saw (3) with a narrow, curved blade makes it a cinch to work between closely spaced branches. A longer, arched pruning saw (4) with larger teeth easily saws big limbs. A pole saw (5) is essentially a handsaw on a stick, extending your reach so you can cut higher branches without leaving the ground.

You may not find this use listed in the manufacturer's literature, but if you're looking for a way to save time and a little back strain when edging your lawn, you might want to try installing a coarse blade and using your reciprocating saw to do the job.

A Reciprocating Saw Gets Down and Dirty

I have an unorthodox use for my trusty reciprocating saw. I attach a medium-length coarse (wood-cutting) or demolition blade to the reciprocating saw and use it to edge my lawn around sidewalks. The blade should be one you don't care much about, and the throat of the saw will plug up with grass and need to be cleaned, but it works and is cheaper than renting or buying a power edger.

To use the reciprocating saw as an edger, hold the saw so that the blade is at about a 45° angle, and run the blade along the edge of the sidewalk.

Patrick J. Derosiers
Denver, Colorado

Plant Ties

If you cut apart all of your old pantyhose, you can make great ties for your plants—and you get a lot of them. The ties are especially good because they stretch and won't rub too much against the tender stems of plants. If you use ties that do rub, diseases can get inside and kill your plants.

Josette Giacobbi
Columbia, South Carolina

Taller plants, such as liatris, usually need stakes. Cut-up pantyhose make good ties.

Make Your Own Garden Cart

I made a garden cart to store all of my tools in. Here's how you can make one: Take a 32- by 36-inch sheet of plywood for the base, framed by 2 x 4s. This base helps keep the tools on the platform from sliding off. Next, build a box using two 1 x 10-inch pine boards that are about 36 inches long and then two pegboard pieces about 14 inches wide and 36 inches long. Take two 1 x 4s and drill 1-inch holes for 30-inch dowel rods. Fasten these 1 x 4s along the top of the pegboard box. The 1 x 4s and dowel rods keep long-handled tools upright. You can put four large casters under the plywood base and paint the wood. (You can adjust the size to fit your needs if you need to.)

Donald Perriguey
Ellington, Missouri

GARDEN TALK

Keep Your Straws

Here's a use for old plastic drinking straws. Cut a 3- to 4-inch length from the straw and trim one end to act as a scooper. This works great for fertilizing potted plants because it's easy to reach under the leaves due to the straw's length and narrow size.

June Garcia
Honokaa, Hawaii

Drinking straws have many gardening-related uses, including fertilizing your potted plants.

An old linoleum knife makes an efficient weeding tool.

Try This!

The best tool I've found for weeding is a crescent-shaped linoleum knife. It should be available from any home improvement store. They are very sharp and the shape helps get the roots of the plants.

Susan Hatton
Pekin, Illinois

A New Way to Water

I recycle my plastic mustard bottles. I just wash them out well and fill them with clean water. They make a handy and adjustable watering device that allows you to add just the right amount of water. If you mix up a batch of water-soluble fertilizer, you can water and fertilize at the same time without worrying about spilling. It's great.

Tito Villareal
Glendale, California

Three-Wheel Barrow Takes a Load Off

Three years ago, my father had his hip removed. Because he was still active, and wanted to work around the house, he made a wheelbarrow that would still be operable without having to lift the handles to move it. He came up with this three-wheeled design by adding an axle and two wheels beneath the back legs of the wheelbarrow. It was a simple project that made use of parts that had been lying around his workshop and garage.

To modify your wheelbarrow, attach an axle beneath the legs of the wheelbarrow with U-style bolts (See photo, left). You may need to drill holes through the legs to attach the U-bolts. Then slide the wheels onto the axles and hold them in place with snap washers and axle caps. The larger the diameter of the wheels, the farther up the wheelbarrow will tip and the easier it will be to roll over rough ground.

Dale A. Reilly
Tucson, Arizona

Parts for this wheelbarrow modification include an axle rod, two U-style bolts with washers and nuts, lockwashers to hold the wheels on the axle, and end caps to cover the ends of the axle. You can find these supplies at most hardware stores.

Using the Short End of the Stick

I took a discarded, worn out yard rake and gave it new life. By simply shortening the handle and grinding the tips off flat, I now have a "wisp rake" to help scoop up leaves and straw.

Phil Duck
Columbia, South Carolina

This "hand rake" has many uses in the yard and garden.

The Other Kind of Shower Ring

I use bathroom shower curtain rings to hold plants to fences so that they don't blow over. As the plants grow, I open the rings a little farther and move them upward on the fence. When the plants die, you can take the rings inside and save them for next year. They last for years and don't hurt your plants at all—plus they're inexpensive.

Martie Busse
Coupeville, Washington

Shower rings can hold plants where you want them, such as against a fence.

GARDEN TALK

Recycled Plant Markers

I recycle my plastic milk and orange juice containers by cutting them into strips with a scissors. I write the names of my plants on the plastic markers with a permanent laundry felt pen. The orange juice strips are very easy to see because of the color. That way I don't have to buy expensive plant markers and I'm recycling my plastic containers.

Dydia Broussard
Crowley, Louisiana

Try a Mason's Trowel

I use a small-sized mason's trowel for weeding, making rows for seeds, and digging. It's very handy and quite versatile.

Robert Bouchard
East Longmeadow, Massachusetts

A mason's trowel does double duty as a weeding tool.

Get a Grip on Gutter Clutter

I've discovered one of the best ways to clean leaves from my gutters. Just use common salad scissors, and you'll be amazed how much better they work than traditional plastic scoops.

Phil Duck
Columbia,
South Carolina

Regular old salad scissors are perfect for conveniently scooping leaves and debris from gutters.

Don't Toss Your Buckets

There are hundreds of uses for good, old 5-gallon buckets. You can use them as forms for concrete, potting soil holders, mini-composters (be sure to drill some holes in it first, otherwise you'll end up with bad, smelly compost), watering buckets for large pets, bulb storage in the winter, a tool caddy, a twine dispenser (drill a hole in the top and feed the end of the twine from the bucket up through the hole), a stepping stool, a place to sit while you work and many more. Check with local companies—they sometimes give them away for free. When you're not using them, they stack and take up little space. (Make sure they're dry, though, before you stack them, otherwise you might have a really hard time pulling them apart.)

Leah Hamilton
Yuma, Arizona

Chapter 10
Watering Techniques

Alongside having good soil, watering well is one of the most important secrets to a healthy garden. Whether you grow indoors or out, keeping track of when and how you water will make a tremendous difference in your plants. While it may not seem very complicated, good watering techniques are vital. Check out these members' ideas on how to get the most out of your water supply and plants.

From the NHGC Staff...

Check Soil Moisture

Make it a practice to dig up some soil from several inches below the soil surface to check water content every week. You may be surprised how dry or how wet your soil is after watering.

Advice *from the* Editor

Stop Scars

Try not to get water on your African violet leaves. If there's more than a 10-degree difference between the temperature of the leaf and the temperature of the water, the leaf will be scarred. Plus, if your water has carbonates in it, it can leave a white film on the leaves.

How and When

If you water your plants, water them deeply and not very often. This will encourage the roots to grow deeper where the soil has more moisture and is cooler. That means you have to water less often and your plants will resist drought better.

Jena Barnett
St. David, Arizona

Let Nature Do the Work

I have an underground irrigation system, but I need to drain it in the fall so that the pipes don't freeze up. I now insert a 5-foot section of soaker hose at the lowest point of my underground pipes. This allows the water to seep away, even when the irrigation system isn't used. Since the pipes freeze from the surface downward, the frost squeezes excess water through the system and out of the soaker hose. I have not had a freeze-up problem since I first tried this idea. It works great!

Gunther Hausen
Newport, Rhode Island

Give Some Back

After I steam vegetables for my meals, I use the water to water my plants with. My plants seem to love it!

Amy Peterson
Minneapolis, Minnesota

From the NHGC Staff...

Place Plants with Similar Moisture Needs Together

Place thirsty plants together and drought-tolerant plants together so that no plant receives too much or too little water. Place less drought-tolerant plants in areas where they are protected from drying winds and hot afternoon sun.

A Moisture Ring

Here's a tip to help make your newly-planted trees and shrubs healthier. To help protect your young trees and shrubs, make a border around them. I buy sewer hose (the kind with small holes punched in it), then dig a trench around my plants. After that, I place the pipe into the trench and cut a large hole in the top of the pipe and fill it with water. The water will slowly seep out around the plant, and make a border at the same time so that you don't get too close with the lawnmower or weed trimmer.

Melvin Church
Linwood, Kansas

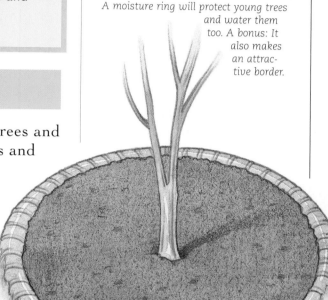

A moisture ring will protect young trees and water them too. A bonus: It also makes an attractive border.

Soaker Hose Success

When you buy a new soaker hose, they can be very stiff and hard to work with. I just use some U-shaped plant markers to hold the hose in place with. (They're exactly the right width to hold the hose.) After a few weeks when the hose has adjusted to its new form and you don't need the "holders," just take them and put them back in the beds with the plants they belong with.

Midge Price
Olympia, Washington

Advice *from the* Editor

Wait Before You Water

Let your water sit for a while before you use it on your plants. That way you can allow it to get to be room temperature—which is better for your plants.

Advice *from the* Editor

Give Them a Little Extra Help

Water your evergreen trees well in the autumn if you live in an area where it freezes in winter. When the ground is frozen, these plants can't absorb water, so they can only use what they stored from the earlier autumn.

No One Has to See How You Water

I run soaker hoses about 6 inches below the soil. They make sure that there's no evaporation and that the plants get all of the water. It encourages the plant roots to grow down to the hose instead of growing right to the top of the soil. The result? My plants hold up better to drought if I'm not able to water when it's dry.

Eileen Bahlmann
Frederika, Iowa

Don't Waste Water

Do you live in an area where it's awfully dry? I use small plastic soda bottles (with pencil-sized holes punched in the sides and bottom of the bottle) buried up to the neck in the ground beside each of my plants. I put lots of mulch around the plant so that only the small bottle top extends above the ground. Add water and food to the bottle, so then it all goes into the soil, right to the plant.

Nancy Bealmear
Hanover, Maryland

From the NHGC Staff...

Testing for Drainage

Run a simple test to see how your soil drains. Dig a hole 18 to 24 inches across and 18 to 24 inches deep. Fill the hole with water. If water disappears from the hole in 10 minutes or less you have sandy soil with fast drainage. If the water takes one hour or more to drain away you have clay soil or a hardpan (an impermeable layer of compacted soil beneath the soil surface) and the soil is poorly drained. There are many acceptable variations between these two extremes.

Keep It Level

If you make a drip irrigation out of PVC pipe, don't bury it—leave it on top of the bed. Then cover it up with mulch. This will make it much easier to maintain if a pipe ever breaks, and you can always move a pipe aside if you need to dig.

Roslyn Hancock
Pleasant Grove, Utah

Pea-Gravel Dry Well Gives Grass a Chance

The main runoff from the drip channels of my house trailer had always caused very bad craters in the soil at the two down-sloped corners. I found a very simple solution. At the worst drip point, I dug a hole approximately 12 inches in diameter and 3 feet deep. Then I filled the hole with pea-gravel from a hardware store. I am pleased to report that last year I had grass move into the eroded space for the first time.

Vincent M. Boreczky
Fennville, Michigan

From the NHGC Staff...

The Circumference of a Plant's Root Mass

Although the rule of thumb used to be that the roots of a plant grew out as far as a tree or shrub's dripline (where water would drip down to the ground from the tips of the branches) studies now show that roots may actually extend even farther than that. Irrigate farther than just between the trunk and the dripline to be sure you're doing a thorough job.

Advice *from the* Editor

No Need for Worry

Sometimes in the heat of the summer on a windy day, your plants will wilt. On days like this, they'll wilt no matter what because of the heat of the day. The plants should recover by the end of the day when it cools off—with no harm done.

Chapter 11
Odds and Ends

This section is filled with tips that didn't quite seem to fit anywhere else in the book—and that's natural because there are so many styles and aspects of gardening. Here you'll find ideas about cutting flowers from your garden, how to keep your annuals going strong, and how to keep your hands clean and healthy. These bits of wisdom are some of the most varied and interesting in this book. Jump in and enjoy!

If you build structures, be sure to check with your local authorities in case you need permits, and so your projects can meet any codes.

Want a Gazebo?

I recycled our old satellite dish into a gazebo. Just make a strong frame out of landscape timbers (or other sturdy lumber) and suspend the dish upside down on top as the roof. Just bolt it into place and paint it. I lined the bottom of the gazebo with old bricks and made walls out of lattice. It's a wonderful way to use an old product and beautify your yard at the same time.

Betty Nunley
Fletcher, Oklahoma

Don't Spray Against the Wind

I've learned that you should never use herbicides, fungicides or insecticides when it's windy outside. Wait for a calm day because the fumes can kill plants, even if they're very far away. (Grapes can be killed that are a mile away!)

Louis McNerney
Port Orange, Florida

From the NHGC Staff...

Bag Out Light

If the best place you can find to dry flowers is in bright light, you can preserve the colors of your blossoms by enclosing each bunch in a roomy paper bag. After the bunch is hung, place a paper bag over the blossoms and staple the open end shut around the stems. Remove the bag after a couple of weeks. Allow the dried blooms to air for a day or two before packing them in storage boxes.

Wheelbarrow-Style Bench Brightens Garden Setting

About five years ago my wife saw a wheelbarrow garden bench in a gardening magazine and wanted to have one someday. I made this bench for her last Christmas. It's my own design and required approximately 150 hours of labor. I am a carpenter/woodworker for a custom millwork shop.

The bench is made from river-recovered heart pine. The entire piece is completely done with joinery—no nails, screws or fasteners—and everything is glued with epoxy. The arm/leg pieces are each one solid piece, with the back supports bent at 15°. They are joined to the main rails with crosslap joints. The crestrail is joined to the back supports by mortise and loose tenon. The seat slats are doweled to the seat supports—not by drilling through but by predrilling the supports, then using spacers and dowel centers to mark the locations on each slat. The slats are attached with epoxy and dowels.

The arm slats are doweled as well. The tricky part is where the slats meet the back support. Each of the top five slats had to be cut at a different compound angle in respect to the angle and radius of the back support top. The backrest members and all remaining frame assembly were done with mortise and tenon joinery. After the bench was assembled I scraped it with a cabinet scraper, then applied an exterior finish.

The wheel is an actual wheelbarrow wheel that I bought from a local antique dealer. It's approximately 100 years old and is the exact size I needed. I repaired and painted the wheel as well as polished the solid brass collars at the ends of the axle. I think it adds a nice touch and it's nice to know I'm reusing a piece of workmanship done by someone else long ago.

This bench is pretty darn comfy to sit in as we admire our hard work in the gardens.

David M. Rose
New Haven, Vermont

Winter Covers

Do you have problems cleaning out the leaves from your groundcovers each spring? I did because the rake would tear out my plants. Then I discovered that if I lay some bird netting on top of my plants, I can just lift it off come spring—no problem!

Kathy Niver
Hebron, Connecticut

Build a Greenhouse

My husband made a great greenhouse for just a little cost. The foundation was made of landscape timbers notched together, log-cabin style, to a height of two timbers. He made the frame out of sturdy PVC pipe, and covered it with corrugated fiberglass. We filled all of the cracks and joints with expanding foam sealer. It's a great place to start seeds in the early spring!

Corrine Brandt
Haltom City, Texas

Make sure your PVC is sturdy enough to hold pots full of soil and plants. What could be more heart-breaking than to find a broken mess one morning?

Cleaning Up

I put a bar of soap in a plastic mesh bag and hang it near my garden hose. This makes for a fast and easy cleanup after a day in the yard and I don't get the inside of my house dirty from my messy hands.

Christine Summers
Levittown, Pennsylvania

An Inexpensive Patio

I made a patio out of recycled bricks that I hauled from the local junkyard. Then I planted some flowers around the edges and used the trunks of fallen trees as edging.

Mary Ann Marino
West Pittsburg, Pennsylvania

Advice *from the* Editor

Balance Your Arrangements

When you make flower arrangements from your cut flowers, it's helpful to keep "balance" in mind. There's real balance that keeps the arrangement from being top-heavy and tipping over, but there's also perceived balance that makes it look just right. One way to keep your arrangement balanced is to use lighter-colored flowers (such as whites or pale pinks) near the top and darker-colored flowers (dark purples or blues) on the bottom. It's a good idea, too, to use fine flowers, such as baby's breath, near the top and larger flowers, such as zinnias, near the bottom.

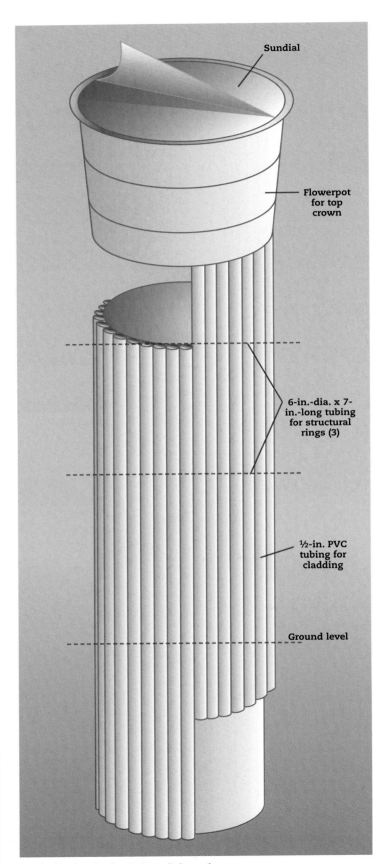

Sundial

Flowerpot
for top
crown

6-in.-dia. x 7-
in.-long tubing
for structural
rings (3)

½-in. PVC
tubing for
cladding

Ground level

Here's the plan for the PVC sundial stand.

PVC Sundial Stand Will Pass the Test of Time

Two years ago I received a beautiful copper sundial as a gift. I searched everywhere for a suitable column to mount the sundial on, but could find nothing.

I decided to make one, so I checked with a local plumbing contractor and secured enough scrap pieces of ½-inch PVC pipe for my project. The core was made from a 21-inch-long piece of 6-inch-diameter PVC cut into three equal lengths for the top, center and bottom. All other pieces, made of ½-inch PVC, were cut into 46-inch lengths and were fastened to the center pieces of 6-inch PVC with all-purpose drywall screws. All holes were drilled and countersunk. Once the assembly of 26 equally spaced tubes was finished, a little caulk took care of the rest— including covering the screw heads.

The top crown on the sundial stand was made from a flowerpot with the bottom removed and the top reinforced, and the sundial was placed on the top. There is approximately 13 inches of column buried in the soil.

Herman C. Martin
Myrtle Beach,
South Carolina

Inside Ornaments

I made an ornament for my wall by taking an old piece of lattice and wiring all of my favorite dried flowers from my garden onto it. The piece of lattice is absolutely gorgeous and has meaning to me because I grew all of the flowers on it. I've got so many flowers that you can't even see the lattice any more!

Jody
Darling
Shelbyville,
Illinois

Keep Your Cut Flowers Longer

I love cut flowers from my garden, but wish they would last for more than a couple of days. I have a technique to keep them fresher. If you want cut flowers from the garden to last longer, just drop an aspirin in the vase of lukewarm water and place the flowers in the refrigerator overnight. (Be sure you don't have any apples or other ripening fruits or vegetables in the refrigerator, though. Ripening fruits and vegetables give off a gas that makes the flowers open and die faster.)

Doris Yoder
Manton, Michigan

Advice *from the* Editor

Organic Matter is Good

Add any type of organic matter (plant-based materials) you can to your soil—especially if your soil has a lot of clay or sand. The organic matter breaks down and adds air spaces so water drains better, but holds water for plants when they need it.

From the NHGC Staff...

On Sounds and Music

Not all special landscape features are visual. The sounds of wind rustling through the trees, the gentle tinkling of bells or wind chimes, or music from an outdoor speaker all add sensual depth to a garden and can help draw attention away from distracting noises from traffic or neighbors. You also can use sound to emphasize a special place, as when you install a small fountain in a water garden or suspend a small wind chime from a limb of your favorite shade tree.

You can easily install weather-resistant speakers under the eaves of your house so you can enjoy music on your deck or patio. Or use a portable stereo as a source of garden music to make weeding go faster or help you hum as you mulch. Look for models built to withstand the hazards of outdoor living.

Keep Your Cannas Going Strong

When I dig out my cannas in the fall, I leave them to dry on my metal patio table (it's the kind that is made of metal wires and looks like a mesh). I lay them on the table and spray with a water hose, then turn them to make sure I get all of the dirt off. The cannas will dry well on the surface because air flows on all sides of them. When they're completely dry, you can store them for the winter.

Shirley Padecki
South Bend, Indiana

Autumn Flowers

To make a pretty centerpiece during autumn, find a nicely shaped gourd. Then hollow it out and coat the inside with melted paraffin wax. Fill the gourd with water and arrange your flowers inside. If it's unstable, you can use some cardboard and florist's putty to keep it sturdy. Use smaller gourds or flowers around the base. It will look so nice during all your celebrations!

Elizabeth Morales
Big Timber, Montana

Winter Color

Michigan winters can be very long and dreary. I decided to brighten mine up by painting the heads of my pampas grass different colors. It really brightened things up and draws the attention of people passing by. My neighbors said they'll try it!

Herschel VanDerKamp
Hamilton, Michigan

If you want more color for a dreary season, go ahead and add it yourself!

Where to Get Help

If you have tough garden questions, don't forget to telephone your Cooperative Extension Service. It is listed in the telephone book under the name of your county. Publications are often available to give you further information about the subject. The agents are experts on what's going on in your specific county.

Marie Hoyer
Lewistown, Montana

Advice *from the* Editor

Help for Your Flowers

If you cut flowers from the garden (or get some from the florist), here's a tip on how to get them to last longer. Each day, simply recut the stem up about a quarter of an inch. This will help the flowers keep absorbing water and stay fresher.

GARDEN TALK

From the NHGC Staff...

Pruning Large Branches

When removing large tree branches, make three cuts to keep the limb from splintering and injuring the trunk:

1 Make the first cut 12 to 24 inches from the branch attachment, sawing until the blade begins to stick or bind: This takes pressure off the branch, preventing binding, for the the next cuts.

2 Make the second cut on top of the branch 1 inch out from the first cut.

3 Remove the stub with your third cut, sawing it off just above the branch collar.

Save Your Geraniums

Do you want to overwinter your annual geraniums (*Pelargonium* spp.)? This is how I overwinter mine. In the fall, just before the first frost, I pull all the geraniums that I want to keep out from the soil. I shake off all of the extra soil so that it only clings to the roots. I place the plant upside down in an old plastic bag. I tie the bag loosely shut on the top so that the plant doesn't fall to the bottom of it. Through the winter, I store it in a dark, dry place and leave it hanging. (I store mine in the basement, but anywhere cool and dry will work.) In spring, pull the plant out of the bag, trim off all of the dead growth, and plant it in potting soil. It will green up rapidly in a sunny spot. Put it outside after all danger of frost has passed.

Karen Buckingham
Hawley, Pennsylvania

Winter Protection

To protect my evergreen shrubs from ice and snow falling off the roof during the winter, I wrap them with chicken wire. I anchor the cage with two or three metal poles hammered into the ground. This allows the shrub to show through the winter and get water, but not damaged. After the ice is gone, I flatten and roll the chicken wire and use it for various things throughout the summer.

Ruth Meyers
Milford,
New Hampshire

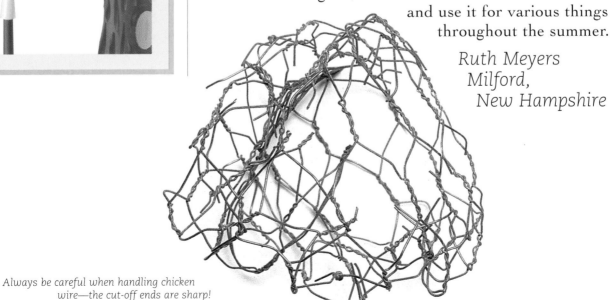

Always be careful when handling chicken wire—the cut-off ends are sharp!

Here's the Scoop: Lay Tarp Before You Dig

The next time you're doing a landscaping project and need to pile dirt on a grassy area, lay a plastic tarp down first. The tarp will keep the dirt from settling into your grass, which makes cleanup difficult and is tough on the lawn. When you remove dirt from the tarp, pull up the tarp corners, which will re-pile the dirt in the center of the tarp—it'll make shoveling easier. (Be careful to keep your shovel from puncturing the tarp as you scoop.) When you're done, you'll be left with a clean grassy area beneath the tarp—no raking required.

Delbert Jessen
Minnetonka, Minnesota

Be Careful!

Be very careful when mowing around trees or using a filament line weed trimmer. Bark wounds may be openings for diseases to enter and cause severe internal destruction and decay. Sometimes the wounds never properly heal over. A 3- to 4-foot circle of mulch around the base of your trees will help provide mower protection.

Marie Hoyer
Lewistown,
Montana

Advice *from the* Editor

Pruning Know-How

If you know when your flowering shrubs bloom, you can know when to prune them. Shrubs that bloom in the spring (forsythias and lilacs, for example) need to make their buds the year before—so prune them right after they bloom. That will give them a chance to make next year's flowers. Shrubs that bloom in the summer (butterfly bushes and hydrangeas, for instance) make their buds as they grow that year—so prune them in early spring before they make their buds.

Along with pruning at the right time, be sure to prune with the right tool.

Besides protecting your trees with a buffer zone, mulch adds a "clean" and neatening look to your yard.

GARDEN TALK

From the NHGC Staff...

Pressing Flowers and Foliage

Blossoms and foliage that are naturally flat, such as pansies and ferns, are fun to dry by pressing. You can use a flower press if you like, but a weighty city phone book will work just as well. Lay the material out in a single layer between the pages, and place the book in a warm place (like the top of your refrigerator) for several weeks. Use a metal spatula to lift the dried blossoms or leaves, and use them to make framed flower arrangements, glue them onto note cards, or use them to decorate wrapped packages. Dried pressed flowers can be preserved indefinitely between laminated sheets of clear plastic—the usual way of making them into lovely bookmarks.

Try this Fertilizer

Instead of using conventional fertilizer/plant food, try using rabbit food! It is a rich source of nitrogen, and it's not poisonous (so you don't have to worry about your junior gardeners putting the pellets in their mouths)!

Stacey Dale
Las Vegas, Nevada

Keep Your Cuts Going

When cutting woody stems, such as hydrangea, from the garden make a slit up the stem. The slit should only be about an inch deep. Then place the stem in warm water in a cool location. The slit in the stem gives the stem more surface area to take up water. (Warm water is more easily taken up by the plant than cold because warm water opens the pores in the plant. Cold water closes the pores.) The cool location helps the plant to recover and harden off so that it can be used in arrangements without the problem of wilting.

Amber Morrow
Maplewood, Minnesota

Drying Flowers

Do you love to save your garden flowers? I've found that one great way is to air-dry them. When air-drying flowers from the garden, layer them so that the heads aren't all packed together. This will allow for better air circulation and less molding. You can also tie flowers with wire or string and hang on hangers. You can hang the hangers easily in a closet or some other warm place to dry.

*Amber
Morrow
Maplewood,
Minnesota*

Pinch and Tuck

Want to get more life out of the bedding plants you buy in those "cell packs?" Here's what I do: Always pinch back bedding plants right after transplanting from a pack. This will make the plants branch out, grow fuller and give you more color for the rest of the year!

*Amy Neigebauer
Owatonna, Minnesota*

Roses are a favorite for drying, but in reality just about any flower will dry well.

Save the Sticks

When I prune large branches and woody brush, I save the stems and main branches. They make great stakes for my garden and they last for several seasons. Plus, they look a lot more natural than expensive bamboo or aluminum poles.

Annie Wood
Roslyn, Pennsylvania

Simple, easily-available materials combine to make this attractive and comfortable garden swing.

In the Swing

This swing design is comfortable, particularly if you raise your arms and rest them on the chain spreader bar above the seat. Cushions also enhance the comfort of the swing, though I removed them here for clarity. Although I used nails to join the boards, you could also use screws. My swing could be built out of any weather-resistant wood such as white oak, teak, redwood or even treated lumber. I used cedar. The chains and hardware needed to hang the swing could vary but should not be skimpy. I used S-hooks where the chains meet to make taking the swing down easy.

Gene P. Schell
Bartonville, Texas

Covering What You Don't Want

Childrens' swingsets grow old and rusty when they're no longer used. To recycle ours, I planted ivy around the poles. The ivy grew and completely covered the frame. It looks so much better—and I can hang hanging baskets from the frame!

Elliot Breuer
San Jose, California

Healing Your Hands

Do you get nicks on your hands in the garden and hate how long it takes for them to heal? I did, until I found out that I could use Preparation-H on all of those little cuts and scrapes I get from gardening. The medicine usually makes the cuts go away overnight.

Tom Cornell
Payson, Arizona

From the NHGC Staff...

What's Your pH?

The term pH refers to a numerical scale (from 1.0 to 14.0) used to describe the acidity or alkalinity of soil. The neutral point on the pH scale is 7.0. A pH reading more than a half point lower (below 6.5) is acidic. A higher reading indicates alkaline soil.

The soil's pH strongly influences the availability of many minerals that plants use as nutrients, including phosphorus, boron, copper and zinc. Some plants prefer rather extreme soil pH levels. Azaleas, blueberries and plants native to the East often thrive in slightly acidic soil. Plants native to the Southwest often prefer alkaline conditions. Most plants, however, prefer a near-neutral pH.

How do you raise your soil's pH? Work agricultural lime into the soil. Use sulfur to lower the pH of alkaline soil. Fertilizers and soil amendments also change the soil's pH over time. Test kits for pH are available at garden centers. Keep one on hand for checking the pH of new garden soil and for monitoring the pH of beds planted with finicky plants.

When edging your lawn with a shovel, save yourself some back strain by using an alternating cutting pattern. In the diagram shown above, the best sequence would be 1, 3, 2, 5, 4, 7, 6. Each section would be shovel width.

Getting the Edge on Edging

To help save your back when edging a lawn with a shovel, it is a good idea never to edge in a straight line. Instead I dig up every other segment by using a pattern of balanced resistance. To understand how important this is, insert a shovel to dig from a corner to a depth of about 6 inches, then skip a space equal to the width of a shovel blade. Next dig up the "in between" section and continue on in this pattern. In other words, from the starting place dig your first section, then the third, then the second, then the fifth, the fourth, the seventh, the sixth, and so on. You'll soon be amazed at how effortless this becomes.

Phil Duck
Columbia, South Carolina

From the NHGC Staff...

Understanding Soil Type and Character

Soil is composed of four main elements: mineral matter, water, air and organic matter. Grains of sand, finely pulverized rock or pebbles are mineral matter. The size, proportions and type of mineral matter give the soil its basic texture, which determines its type. Broadly defined, the four soil types are sand, silt, loam and clay.

- **Sandy soil** is light and easy to dig, warms quickly in the spring and is rich in oxygen. However, sandy soil doesn't hold much moisture or many plant nutrients.

Sandy soil.

- **Silty soil** has a lighter texture than clay but is heavier than sand. Small silt particles travel easily in water, so soil in low places near rivers and streams often has a silty character. Poor drainage and surface crusting are the main problems you will have when gardening in silty soil.

Silty soil.

- **Loam** is the term used to describe soil with a good balance of clay, silt and sand, and a generous amount of organic matter. It is the type of soil everyone wants to have.

Loam.

- **Clay soil** is heavy and difficult to dig and has little pore space for oxygen. Clay often contains plenty of plant nutrients, but the nutrients may be not be available to plants because of the soil's tight texture. Clay soil tends to stay wet for a long time after heavy rains, and may drain poorly. When clay dries out it becomes rock hard. It is encouraging to know that clay soil becomes terrific garden soil if a sufficient amount of organic matter is added.

Clay soil.

Glossary

Acid soil Any soil with a pH reading below 7.0 on a scale of 1 to 14; the lower the reading, the more acid the soil. Most garden plants prefer slightly acid to neutral soil. See pH.

Alkaline soil Any soil with a pH reading above 7.0 on a scale of 1 to 14; the higher the reading, the more alkaline the soil. See pH.

Annual A plant that completes its entire life cycle in one season.

Aphid A small sucking insect, usually pale green, gray or black. They are small and pear shaped, and appear in great numbers on young plant growth. You can recognize them by the fact that they secrete a sticky fluid called honeydew, which also attracts ants. Control aphids by knocking them off the plants with a hard stream of cold water or by spraying with insecticidal soap.

Bacillus thuringiensis (Bt) A species of bacteria that attacks caterpillars. Some kinds attack other pests, such as Japanese beetles and grasshoppers.

Beneficial insects Insects that help rather than hinder gardening efforts. They might pollinate, eat harmful insects, or may break down plant material in the soil, and release nutrients.

Biennial A plant that takes two years to complete its life cycle, growing leafy growth the first season, then flowering in its second season before dying.

Bolting The formation of flowering stalks, especially on plants grown for their leaves or roots, lowering harvest quality.

Borer A pest that bores into the stems of plants, usually a larva such as a grub, caterpillar or maggot. Symptoms often include an entrance hole and wilt on stem portions beyond. They can be controlled by digging out the pest, injecting an appropriate botanical or microbial insecticide, or by pruning the plant below the

damage and destroying it with the pest intact.

Bulb An underground part of the plant that stores energy. It is made of layers of fleshy and dried leaf bases and has roots attached to its bottom.

Bulbil Small bulb-like organs attached to a plant. Underground it's called a bulblet.

Climber A vine that climbs on its own, using twining, gripping pads, tendrils or some other method of attaching itself to structures or other plants.

Companion planting Intermixing different crops to benefit one or more of them. Some people plant roses and chives together, for example.

Compost Decayed vegetable matter that looks like soil. It is used to improve the texture and fertility of garden soil.

Corm A bulb-like, underground storage structure. Crocus and gladiolus grow from corms.

Cover crop A crop grown to occupy or improve the soil in a part of the garden that is not currently producing.

Crop rotation Planting different kinds of plants in the same spot over different years. It helps balance soil nutrients and slows the cycle of pests and diseases.

Cross-pollination When one plant pollinates another, different plant. The seeds will grow into a plant that looks different than the parents.

Crown The base of a plant, where stem and bud join, usually, but not always at ground level. Many perennials grow from crowns.

Cutting Removing a part of a stem or root so it can develop into a new plant.

Cutworm The caterpillar of several kinds of moths. They emerge from the soil at night and "cut down"

seedlings, then devour them, leaving no evidence beyond the severed stem. To stop them, try putting 1-inch-tall collars around the stem of newly set transplants so that the cutworms can't get to them.

Damping off A group of fungal diseases that attack seedlings and make the stem wither at the soil line, causing the plant to topple over. There is no cure for affected plants, but you can prevent the disease by growing the seedlings in a warm, bright, airy location. Avoid overwatering, too.

Division Breaking or cutting apart of the crown of a plant to make additional plants.

Espalier Growing trees supported by structures, to form a narrow hedge or fence. Espaliers are often trained to grow flat along the south face of a stone or brick wall so the wall holds heat overnight, making the fruit mature early.

Fertilizer Any material containing good amounts of plant nutrients, especially nitrogen (N), phosphorus (P) and postassium (K—also called potash). Fertilizers are required to have the analysis of these three nutrients printed on the container.

Fungicide Any material capable of killing fungi. Sulfur and copper sulfate are two common fungicides.

Germination The sprouting stage of a seed.

Green manure A crop grown only so you can turn it under. This improves the soil by adding organic matter.

Hardening off The process of gradually exposing seedlings started indoors to outdoor conditions before transplanting.

Herbaceous A plant that dies to the ground in winter.

Herbicide A material that kills plants, generally weeds. Some soaps have herbicidal properties.

Humidity The amount of water in the air. Most houseplants like high humidity.

Hybrid A plant grown from seed crossed from two distinctly different plants.

Insecticidal soap Specially formulated soap that kills an insect, but is relatively harmless to plants.

Insecticide A material that kills insects. There are numerous powders that are toxic to insects, as well as biodegradable chemicals such as soaps.

Interplanting Mixing several different plants in the same planting space. You can do this for aesthetic reasons, pest and disease control or simply to raise the yield per square foot. See also companion planting.

Latin name The scientific name of a plant. The Latin name consists of two parts: the first, called the genus name, states the genus to which the plant belongs. The second name, called the species name, describes the species to which the plant belongs.

Lime A rock powder that is used to raise the pH (that is, to decrease the acidity) of soils.

Maturity, days to For plants generally started indoors, the number of days from setting of transplants in the open garden until the first harvest. For crops sown direct in the garden, the number of days from seedling emergence to the first harvest.

Mealybug An insect that sucks plant juices. It covers itself in a white, cottony substance.

Nitrogen A major plant nutrient that's important for plant foliage.

NPK An acronym for the three major plant nutrients contained in manure, compost and fertilizers. N is for nitrogen, P for phosphorus, and K for potassium.

Nutrient Any mineral that's essential for plant growth.

Nutrient deficiency When plants don't do well because they don't have enough of a particular nutrient. Yellowish leaves are often a symptom.

Organic matter That portion of the soil comprised of living, or once living, organisms or their remains.

Parterre A kind of formal garden design wherein geometrically arranged beds are planted with edgings and decorative arranged crops, whether ornamental or edible, or both. See also Potager.

Pathogen Anything that causes a plant disease.

Peat Partially decomposed mosses and sedges harvested from bogs and used as a component of soil-less potting mixes.

Peat pots Planting pots made from compressed peat. These are used for plants that don't like to be disturbed because the young plants roots will grow through the walls of the pot.

Perennial Any plant that lives more than three years. Perennials can be herbaceous or woody.

Perlite A white, porous, material that is used to improve the drainage of potting mixes. See also vermiculite.

pH A symbol for the acid-alkaline balance of the soil. The balance is expressed as a number from 1 to 14, with 7 considered neutral. A pH of 6 is acidic while a pH of 8 is alkaline. Higher numbers are more alkaline, lower numbers more acidic.

Phosphorus A major plant nutrient. Phosphorus is sometimes associated with flowering.

Potager A French term applied to food gardens that are decorative as well as merely functional. See also Parterre.

Potassium A major plant nutrient associated with the strength of roots and stems.

Pruning The removal of plant parts to improve the health, appearance or productivity of the plant.

Rhizome A horizontal stem, usually underground, from which grow both leaves and roots. Usually persistent from year to year. Tall bearded iris grow from rhizomes.

Rootbound A situation where plant roots have filled the container where they grow. Plants that are highly rootbound quit growing.

Slug A snail-like creature that eats plant parts. It crawls along the soil and leaves slimy trails behind it.

Soil-less mix Any potting mix that is made without soil. Some common components include peat, bark, coconut fiber, vermiculite, perlite and sand.

Succession planting Replanting a crop at intervals throughout the growing season to get longer harvest.

Topdressing Applying fertilizer to the surface of the soil around established plantings.

Tuber An underground plant part that stores nutrients. It can either be part of the stem or the roots. Stem tubers make buds on their surface where shoots may grow from the following season; root tubers sprout from the point at which they were attached to the stem of the parent plant. Dahlias and potatoes are tubers.

Vermiculite A gray, mica-like material that is used to improve the drainage of potting mixes. See also perlite.

Whitefly A white, fly-like insect that sucks the juices from plants.

Plant Hardiness Zone Map

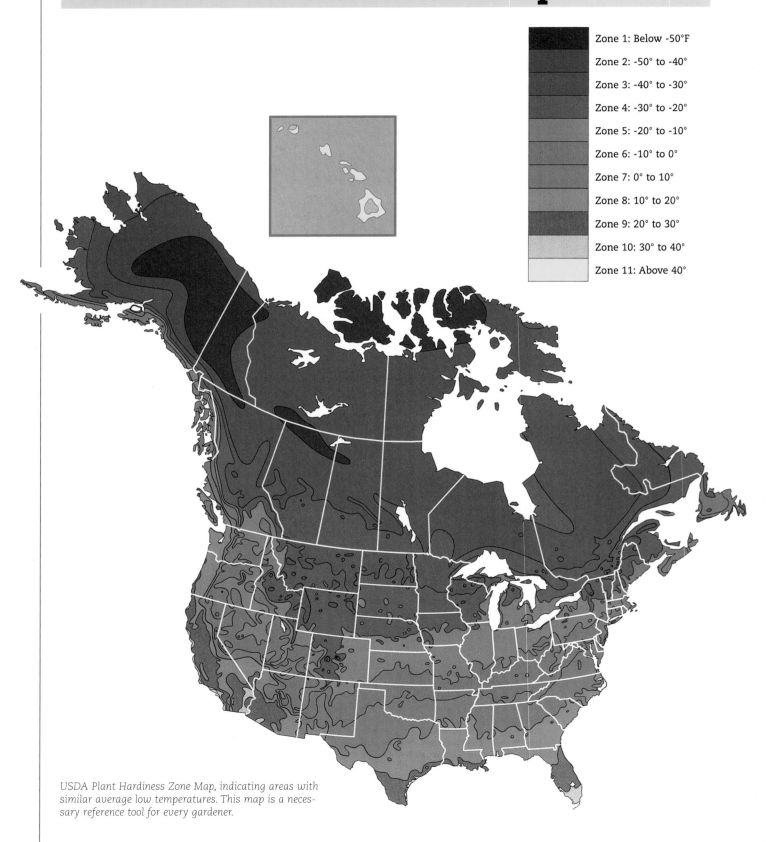

Zone 1: Below -50°F
Zone 2: -50° to -40°
Zone 3: -40° to -30°
Zone 4: -30° to -20°
Zone 5: -20° to -10°
Zone 6: -10° to 0°
Zone 7: 0° to 10°
Zone 8: 10° to 20°
Zone 9: 20° to 30°
Zone 10: 30° to 40°
Zone 11: Above 40°

USDA Plant Hardiness Zone Map, indicating areas with similar average low temperatures. This map is a necessary reference tool for every gardener.

Index

A

African violets, 132
Ajuga, 88
Amaryllis, 113
Angel's trumpet, 91
Ants, 39
Aphids, 34
Arbor, 27

B

Bananas, 73
Barrels, 108
Bats, 6
Beans, climbing, 19, 20
Bees, 14, 15, 30
Bench, 139
Biennial, 63
Birdbath, 10, 14
Bird feeder, 8, 13, 15
Birdhouse, 9, 11
Birds, 12, 30, 36, 37
Black-eyed Susan, 15
Black-eyed Susan vine, 21
Bluebirds, 13
Bottles, 56
Bowling balls, 80
Buckets, 129
Bulbs, protecting, 31

C

Cabbage moths, 32, 38
Cannas, 144
Canvas, 105
Cardinal climber, 26
Carrots, 48
Cats, 33
Cedar mulch, 72
Chickadees, 13
Chopsticks, 59
Christmas lights, 22
Cinnamon, 39
Clematis, 21, 96
Cockscomb, 14
Coffee filters, 104
Coldframe, 59, 62
Compost, making, 69, 71, 73
Compost pile, making, 68
Cookie sheet, 102
Coreopsis, 88
Corn, protecting, 35, 36, 38, 41
Corncobs, 72
Cover cropping, 70
Cucumber beetles, 40
Cucumbers, 44, 50
Cut flowers, 143, 145, 148
Cuttings, 57, 82
Cutworms, 33
Cypress vine, 26

D

Dahlberg daisy, 98
Daylily, 88
Devil's ivy, 104
Diaper pails, 67
Dill, 45
Drainage, 104, 134
Dry streambeds, 93